D1313062

913 000 00021501

DO-IT-YOURSELF
WORKSHOP

LONDON BOROUGH OF HACKNEY	
913 000 00021501	
HJ	13-Nov-2009
643.7	£5.99

DO-IT-YOURSELF
WORKSHOP

THE EXPERT'S GUIDE TO TOOLS AND TECHNIQUES

CONSULTANT:
JOHN McGOWAN

AUTHORS:
MIKE COLLINS, DAVID HOLLOWAY, BRENDA LEGGE, DIANE CARR

SPECIAL PHOTOGRAPHY:
COLIN BOWLING

LORENZ BOOKS

This edition is published by Lorenz Books, an imprint of Anness Publishing Ltd, Hermes House,
88–89 Blackfriars Road, London SE1 8HA; tel. 020 7401 2077; fax 020 7633 9499

www.lorenzbooks.com; www.annesspublishing.com

If you like the images in this book and would like to investigate using them for publishing, promotions or advertising, please visit
our website www.practicalpictures.com for more information.

UK agent: The Manning Partnership Ltd; tel. 01225 478444; fax 01225 478440; sales@manning-partnership.co.uk
UK distributor: Grantham Book Services Ltd; tel. 01476 541080; fax 01476 541061; orders@gbs.tbs-ltd.co.uk
North American agent/distributor: National Book Network; tel. 301 459 3366; fax 301 429 5746; www.nbnbooks.com
Australian agent/distributor: Pan Macmillan Australia; tel. 1300 135 113; fax 1300 135 103; customer.service@macmillan.com.au
New Zealand agent/distributor: David Bateman Ltd; tel. (09) 415 7664; fax (09) 415 8892

Publisher: Joanna Lorenz
Managing editor: Judith Simons
Project editor: Felicity Forster
Editor: Ian Penberthy
Designer: Paul Calver
Illustrator: Peter Bull
Photographer: Colin Bowling
Photography consultant: Simon Gilham
Technical assistant: John Ireland
Production controller: Claire Rae

ETHICAL TRADING POLICY

Because of our ongoing ecological investment programme, you, as our customer, can have the pleasure and reassurance of
knowing that a tree is being cultivated on your behalf to naturally replace the materials used to make the book you are holding.
For further information about this scheme, go to www.annesspublishing.com/trees

© Anness Publishing Ltd 2003, 2008

All rights reserved. No part of this publication may be reproduced, stored in
a retrieval system, or transmitted in any way or by any means, electronic,
mechanical, photocopying, recording or otherwise, without the
prior written permission of the copyright holder.

A CIP catalogue record for this book is
available from the British Library.

PUBLISHER'S NOTE

The authors and the publisher have made every effort to ensure that all instructions contained in this book are accurate
and safe, and cannot accept liability for any resulting injury, damage or loss to persons or property, however it may arise.
If in doubt as to the correct procedure to follow for any home improvements task, seek professional advice.

Contents

INTRODUCTION

Whether you are faced with a fairly simple job, such as decorating a small bedroom, installing cabinets and shelves or repairing a fence, or something far more ambitious, such as adding a porch or cladding a ceiling or even a whole room, having the right tools and materials for the job, and knowing how to use them will help make everything go smoothly.

MAKE YOUR MARK

Houses and apartments, converted barns and tiny studios are, on their own, merely structures of wood, glass, concrete and masonry. They spring into life and blossom only when the personality of the occupant is stamped upon them. Where you live should be how you live; it is more than just a place to eat and sleep. It should be a microcosm of your whole lifestyle in terms of created space, room design, colour schemes, furniture, lighting, garden layout and all that goes with loving and caring for the home.

For this to be true, we need to put in a lot of time thinking about, experimenting with, and enhancing our own environments, and much of this is possible with relatively few skills.

The most important thing to remember is that do-it-yourself is a practical and deeply satisfying pursuit, which fosters craftsmanship and pride in one's environment through practical achievement.

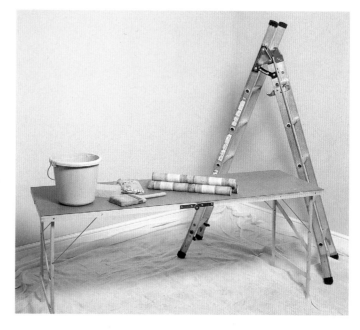

BUILD A TOOL KIT

Being a do-it-yourselfer means having a grasp of a variety of skills that, in the past, would have been the preserve of qualified tradesmen. Today, those tradesmen still exist, but a broad spectrum of amateurs gain great satisfaction and make considerable savings by doing many jobs themselves. Whatever your current level of skill, provided you have a practical turn of mind and are prepared to make the effort to learn how a job is done, you should be able to achieve good results.

LEFT A jigsaw is necessary when you want to cut curves and circles in wood.

ABOVE Preparation for household jobs such as wallpapering can take longer than actually doing the work, but it is absolutely essential. Before you start, clear the room to ensure that you have plenty of space, and put down protective dust sheets (drop cloths).

Among the most important aspects of any job is having the right tools and understanding how to use them properly. One of the objects of this book is to show you just that; the tools described will allow you to carry out a wide variety of do-it-yourself tasks.

Most do-it-yourselfers will assemble a tool kit over a long period of time, beginning perhaps

with a hammer, a saw and a screwdriver or two, then adding new items as they are needed.

As experience and competence grow, more complex and skilled tasks may be tackled and the necessary tools purchased. This gradual enlargement of the tool kit is easy on the pocket.

The more dedicated do-it-yourselfers may even extend their interest in practical matters to a hobby, such as cabinet-making or wood carving, that requires the setting up of a home workshop, complete with machinery and special hand tools. No matter how many tools you buy, always go for the best you can afford; cheap tools rarely last.

MATERIAL FACTS

Along with the right tools, you must have the right materials for any task you tackle. Knowing what you need is just as important as knowing how to do the job. Today, many stores cater specifically for do-it-yourselfers, selling raw materials in quantities that suit smaller jobs; and many manufacturers have developed products that are easier to use by the amateur. All, however, can produce a professional result.

DEVELOP YOUR SKILLS

Specialized skills, such as bricklaying and carpentry, do need the experience of actually handling the tools and materials regularly to gain manual dexterity, and the best way to obtain this experience is to do a few outdoor jobs that are not particularly crucial. Repairing a fence or wall, perhaps laying a few paving slabs, or building a small tool shed or garden frame will help you develop skills remarkably quickly and boost your confidence. As confidence grows, it feeds the imagination, and in a short time, projects for inside the home begin to take shape in the mind.

Beginners should seek as much advice as possible from experienced professionals, or at least read up on the particular project or task in mind so that the more common pitfalls can be avoided. If, on reflection, a job seems too difficult, knowing how it is done can be very useful when employing a professional.

Many colleges offer evening classes where, for a modest sum, the novice can learn carpentry, brickwork and a variety of general do-it-yourself skills. These are worth investigating and can be very rewarding. The advantage of doing something

ABOVE FAR LEFT The most commonly used clamp in the workshop is the G-clamp.

ABOVE LEFT Mixing your own concrete requires careful measurement of the constituent parts.

ABOVE Although costly, a guillotine jig-type tile cutter gives excellent results.

BELOW A tool board displays your tools neatly and makes it obvious when one is missing.

yourself is that your time is free, so never rush a job; haste encourages mistakes, leads to disappointment, and can be expensive in the cost of spoiled materials.

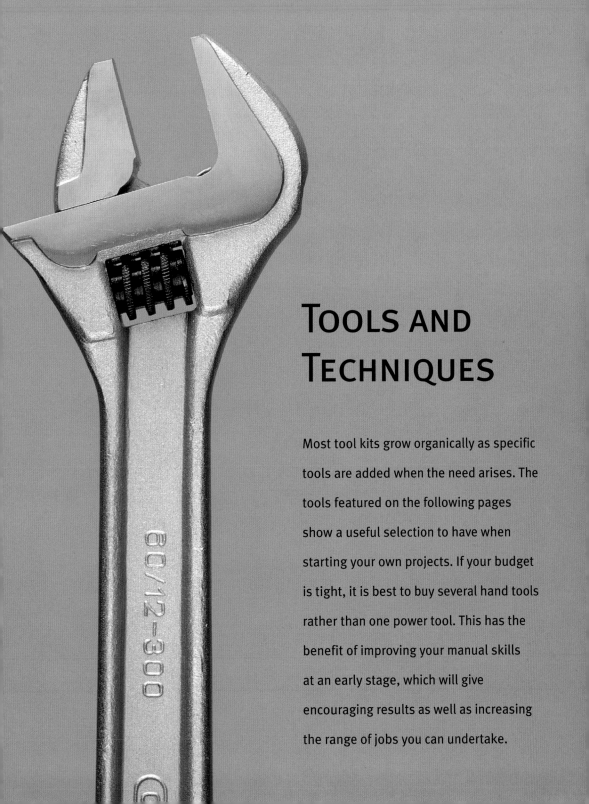

Tools and Techniques

Most tool kits grow organically as specific tools are added when the need arises. The tools featured on the following pages show a useful selection to have when starting your own projects. If your budget is tight, it is best to buy several hand tools rather than one power tool. This has the benefit of improving your manual skills at an early stage, which will give encouraging results as well as increasing the range of jobs you can undertake.

SAFETY EQUIPMENT

A complete book could be devoted to the subject of safety in the home, and there is a wide range of equipment designed to minimize our capacity for hurting ourselves. Nevertheless, there is one requirement that we cannot buy, without which all that equipment is virtually useless, namely concentration. This is particularly important when working alone.

AWARENESS

Concentration is essential when using any form of power tool, especially a saw, where one slip can mean the loss of a finger, or worse. The dangers of accidents involving electricity are well documented, as are those involving falls from ladders, spillages of toxic materials, and burns and injuries caused by contact with fire or abrasive surfaces. In almost every case, there is a loss of concentration, coupled with poor work practices and inadequate protective clothing or equipment. So, although the items shown here are all useful, concentrating on what you are doing is the best advice to prevent accidents from occurring around the home and workshop.

BASIC EQUIPMENT

Overalls are a good investment because they not only protect clothing, but also most are designed to be close-fitting to prevent accidental contact with moving machinery. Industrial gloves,

ABOVE Rubber knee pads for floor work avoid damage to both the floor and person.

LEFT The "bump" cap is more stylish than the hard hat and will cope with most accidents.

although not worn by those engaged in fine work, can provide very useful protection against cuts and bruises when doing rougher jobs, such as fencing and garden work. Similarly, safety boots should be worn when heavy lifting or the use of machinery is involved. They are essential when using a chainsaw.

Knee pads are necessary for comfort when laying a floor, stripping one for varnishing or carrying out any other job that requires a lot of kneeling. They will also protect the wearer from injury if a nail or similar projection is knelt on accidentally. Finally, a bump cap is worth considering. This will protect the head from minor

FAR LEFT Wear overalls for protection when painting and decorating.

ABOVE LEFT Gloves are essential when handling rough materials.

LEFT Safety boots with steel toe caps will protect your feet.

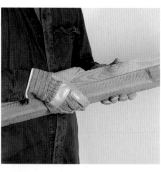

injuries and bumps, but is not so cumbersome as the hard hat required on building sites.

It is inevitable that minor cuts and abrasions will occur at some point so a basic first aid kit is another essential for the home or workshop.

AIRBORNE DANGERS

When you are working with wood, the most common airborne danger is dust, mainly from sawing and sanding. This can do long-term damage to the lungs. Many do-it-yourself enthusiasts do not do enough work to warrant a workshop dust extractor, but it would be worth considering if funds allowed. Such a device can be wall-mounted or portable. In the latter case, it can be moved around the house or workshop to suit any tool in use.

A simple face mask, however, will offer adequate protection for occasional jobs. These can also be purchased for protection against fumes, such as from solvents, which can be very harmful. Dust, of course, also affects the eyes, so it is worth investing in a pair of impact-resistant goggles, which will protect the wearer from both fine dust and

LEFT Keeping a basic first aid kit is a common and wise precaution even before any do-it-yourself work is envisaged. It should always be prominently displayed for people unfamiliar with the workshop.

flying debris. Full facial protection is available in the form of a powered respirator for those working in dusty conditions over long periods.

Excessive noise is another airborne pollutant that can be dangerous over a long period. Woodworking machinery, such as planers and circular saws, is often the culprit. Earplugs are the simplest solution and can be left in the ears over a long period. If you need to be able to hear between short bouts of working, ear protectors are the

answer. These can be worn in conjunction with other facial protection quite easily.

PRACTICAL TIP

• Perhaps the most basic advice is to never work alone with machinery and if it is possible always have a friend or colleague nearby to help. If there is no telephone, having a mobile (cell) phone is handy in the workshop.

ABOVE Ear defenders are good for really loud noise but should be used sparingly.

ABOVE Dust extraction is the first line of defence in the workshop.

ABOVE A simple face mask can filter out the worst dust pollution.

ELECTRICAL AND LADDER SAFETY

Most safety considerations concerning the use of power tools will be set out by the manufacturers in the operating instructions, so it is essential always to read the manuals on purchase and follow these to the letter. Using ladders, however, needs some direct input from the user by way of common sense, since no two situations are ever the same.

ELECTRICAL SAFETY

Some tools have removable switches that allow the user to immobilize the tool and prevent any unauthorized use. Provisions for the use of padlocks are also common on machinery, and it is wise to buy tools with such facilities.

To safeguard against electrocution, which can occur if the power cord is faulty or is cut accidentally, the ideal precaution is a residual current device (RCD). This is simply plugged into the main supply socket (electrical outlet) before the power cord and will give complete protection to the user. Extension cords can be purchased with automatic safety cut-outs and insulated sockets (receptacles) and are ideal for both outside and inside work.

The danger of electrocution or damage caused by accidentally drilling into an existing cable or pipe can be largely prevented by using an electronic pipe and cable detector, which will locate and differentiate between metal pipes, wooden studs and live wires through plaster or concrete to a depth of approximately 50mm (2in). These are not too expensive and will be very useful around the home.

The danger of fire is ever present in both the home and workshop, so a fire extinguisher (possibly two or three) is necessary for every do-it-yourself enthusiast. It should be wall-mounted in plain view and tested and serviced regularly.

ABOVE AND LEFT Pipe and cable detectors give information which can largely eliminate any danger from electrocution.

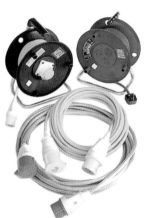

ABOVE Proper cable reels and insulated sockets protect the user from electrocution.

ABOVE A fire extinguisher is absolutely essential in the workshop or at home. Make sure the one you have is adequate for the size and type of workshop, and the type of fire source.

LEFT A simple circuit breaker can save a life.

ABOVE A ladder platform will ensure a firm footing, especially if heavy footwear is worn.

RIGHT Keeping tools on a stable surface when working at heights adds to your personal safety.

BELOW RIGHT A ladder attachment over the ridge of a roof improves safety and avoids damage to the roof covering.

BELOW Make sure that your ladder is secure at ground level. This is one of the most important steps to safe working practice.

Slipping and falling

Steps and ladders can be hazardous, so make sure they are in good condition. Accessories to make a ladder safer to use include the roof hook, which slips over the ridge for safety; the ladder stay, which spreads the weight of the ladder across a vertical surface, such as a wall to prevent slippage; and the standing platform, which is used to provide a more comfortable and safer surface to stand on. The last often has a ribbed rubber surface and can be attached to the rungs of almost all ladders. Even more stable is the moveable workstation or a board or staging slung between two pairs of steps or trestles. These can often be used with a safety rail, which prevents the operator from falling even if a slip occurs.

ABOVE RIGHT A moveable workstation simplifies the whole process.

RIGHT Platforms supported by trestles are the safest way to paint from a height.

Practical tips

• Never over-reach when working on steps or a ladder; climb down and reposition it.

• Never allow children or pets into areas where power tools or strong solvents are being used.

• Do not work when you are overtired. This causes lapses in concentration, which can lead to silly and/or dangerous mistakes.

• Keep the work environment tidy. Power cords should not be walked on or coiled up tightly, because it damages them internally. Moreover, trailing cords can be a trip hazard and long extension cords can be prone to overheating.

MEASURING AND MARKING

Accurate measuring and marking out are very basic but essential skills for the do-it-yourself enthusiast to master. Time spent on perfecting them is never wasted. The golden rule is to measure twice and cut once. Buy some good quality tools – poor measuring and marking devices can lose their accuracy very quickly and spoil your work.

HOW TO MEASURE

There are dozens of types of flat, rigid rules for marking out, most of which are calibrated in both metric and imperial units. They may be wood or steel, although some cheaper varieties are plastic. Where curves are involved, greater accuracy will be achieved with a flexible steel rule or even a retractable steel tape, which can be bent around the work.

The T-square is useful for marking out large sheets of manufactured board such as plywood, MDF (medium-density fibreboard) or blockboard. Remember, however, that it must be used on a perfectly straight edge to give a 90-degree line across the sheet. Any small discrepancy will be greatly magnified across the sheet width and even more so along the length.

FITTING PRE-MADE STRUCTURES

When fitting previously-assembled cabinets or shelving to a wall, the most accurate method is to mark out the wall using a spirit level. Do not rely on existing lines, such as architraves (trims) around doors, picture rails or skirting (base) boards, as these may not be truly horizontal.

Where you need to mark off a series of equal spacings, simply set a pair of dividers or callipers to the correct distance, using a flat wooden or steel rule, and step off the divisions.

Transferring measurements from one point to another can also be done with a straightedge, and although this is very similar to a heavy steel rule, the bevelled edge gives it the added advantage of being very easy to cut or to mark against.

When marking out for fine work, a marking knife, with a bevel on one side of the blade only, is the tool to use. Such knives can be obtained with bevels on either side and are well worth having.

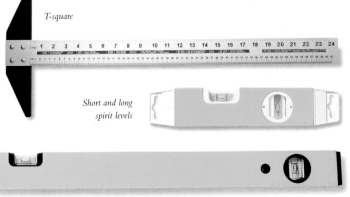

T-square

Short and long spirit levels

Straightedge

Combination square

Measuring tape

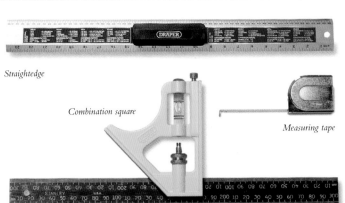

CONVERTING MEASUREMENTS

On small work in particular, never be tempted to convert from metric to imperial or vice-versa. Some quite large errors can occur with standard conversions. Always work in the unit specified.

Sliding bevel

Try square

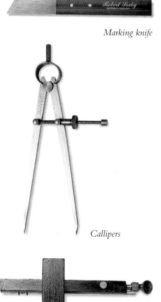

Marking knife

Callipers

Mortise gauge

MARKING OUT

Never use a magic marker or a ballpoint pen when marking out, since the marks are virtually impossible to remove and will spoil your work.

ABOVE Use a carpenter's pencil, pencil, or chinagraph for marking measurements.

MARKING JOINTS

This does need a fair degree of accuracy, so the first thing to ascertain is that your prepared wood is flat and square, which is done with a combination square or a try square. Either of these tools should be slid down the length of the timber to be cut to ensure its uniformity and squareness.

For marking out a mortise, use a mortise gauge and set the points to the width of the chisel you intend to use to cut the mortise, not from a rule. This is far more accurate, as well as being much more convenient.

For marking angles on a piece of square timber, especially if they are to be repeated, such as when setting out treads for a staircase, use a sliding bevel.

A good alternative for marking frequently repeated angles, which are encountered in projects such as staircases, is to make up a jig or template that can be laid on to the stringer (the long diagonal part of the staircase) and mark the treads accordingly. Most workshops keep a range of templates made in hardboard or perspex.

FAR LEFT Use a try square for marking right angles. Keep it clean and make sure the blade is not loose. It can be used with a pencil or a marking knife as required.

LEFT Use a mortise gauge to scribe directly on to the wood. The two steel pins of the mortise gauge are independently adjustable on accurate brass slides, while the sliding stock runs against the face of the work. There is a single pin on the opposite side for marking a single scribed line, used to gauge thickness.

Drills and Bits

These come in a bewildering array of sizes and types but just a few are all that are needed for the home workshop, such as dowel bits for flat-bottomed holes; flat bits, which work with a scraping action and cut large holes very rapidly; and the ordinary twist bit that is used for making small holes and for starting screws. Beware of buying cheap sets of drill bits.

Drills

Accurate drilling is an important do-it-yourself technique, and it is much easier with a hand-held power drill and even more so with a bench-mounted pillar drill.

Drilling by hand with a carpenter's brace still has a place and a hand drill is useful for smaller jobs, especially in sites far removed from electric power. However, even in these circumstances, the cordless power drill has largely overcome the difficulty of needing a source of electric power.

Cordless drill/driver

This is worth its weight in gold in situations without power, and it is particularly safe near water. This hand-held power tool is rechargeable and usually comes with a spare battery. The variable torque and speed settings make it ideal for doubling as a screwdriver. Although generally not as powerful as a mains-powered drill, it is more than adequate for most jobs. Use it for drilling clearance holes for screws, fitting and removing screws, and drilling holes for dowels.

Practical tip

• Never interfere with the centre-point of a drill, if it has one, as this will almost certainly affect its concentricity and effectiveness.

Heavier work, especially that which involves using flat bits or Forstner bits for removing very large areas of wood, is best undertaken with a mains-powered electric drill to save time and avoid constant recharging of the battery.

Cordless drill

Hand drill

Carpenter's brace

Pillar drill

Plug cutter

Counterbore or 3-in-1 bit

Countersink

Twist bit *Dowel bit*

Boring bit

Flat bit

Auger bit *Forstner bit*

PILLAR DRILLS

When using a pillar drill to bore holes that pass through the wood, place a piece of scrap wood beneath the workpiece so that the bit will emerge cleanly and not splinter the surface. Always run a pillar drill at the correct speed, as shown on the tool. This will always be slower for large-diameter drills and faster for smaller ones.

VARIETIES OF BIT

Great advances have also been made in the pattern of drill bits. For example, there are bits designed for setting dowels. Dowel jointing is often used in projects built with manufactured boards, such as chipboard and plywood, and the bits produce flat-bottomed holes.

There are also flat bits that work with a scraping action, cutting large holes very rapidly, although these are not as accurate as conventional twist bits. The latter are used for making small holes in wood, metal and other rigid materials. For the home worker on a limited budget, an adjustable bit is a good investment, but these can only be used in a hand brace. Engineering bits can all be used in woodwork.

DRILLING ACCESSORIES

Plug cutters are useful additions to any workshop, especially when quality work is undertaken. The cutter is fitted in a pillar drill and used to remove plugs from a piece

ABOVE Many drill bits can be sharpened with a specialized grinding attachment designed to be run off a hand-held power drill.

of scrap wood. The plugs are then glued into holes in the workpiece to conceal fixing screws. Most cutters come with a special matching bit that bores a screw clearance hole and plug countersink in one operation.

Another common drilling accessory is the countersink bit. This allows the head of a screw to be set flush with the surface of the wood. Again, this is best used in a pillar drill with a depth stop to ensure accuracy.

Forstner bits are designed to drill large, flat-bottomed holes that do not pass through the wood, such as holes that might be needed to fit kitchen cabinet hinges. The bits will drill deep holes accurately, even in the end grain of timber, which is usually very difficult.

Screws and Screwdrivers

The holding power of screws is much greater than that of nails, and screwed work can easily be taken apart again without damage to any of the components, unless of course it is also glued. Driving screws does take longer than nailing and is also more expensive, but it will give the appearance of quality and craftsmanship to most work.

TYPES OF SCREW

The most frequently used wood screws are made of mild steel or brass, often with countersunk heads that may be flat or raised. There are many different plated finishes available, ranging from chrome, used for internal fixings such as mirrors, to zinc, which will resist rust.

Brass screws will not rust at all and are commonly used in timbers such as oak, where steel would cause blue staining due to the tannic acid in the sap.

SCREW SIZES AND HEAD PATTERNS

There are various types of screw head used for both hand and power driving. The most common in woodworking is the slot-head screw, followed by the Phillips head and the Pozidriv, both of which have a cross pattern in the head to take the screwdriver blade. A small selection of slot-head, Phillips and Pozidriv screwdrivers will cover most needs. Slot-head screwdriver blades can be shaped on a grindstone to restore their condition if necessary. Never use a screwdriver that is too small, as you will ruin the blade and the screw. Screw sizes are complex, combining the diameter (gauge) and the length: for example, "inch-and-a-half eight" describes a screw that is 1½in (40mm) long and gauge 8.

There is no need to delve too deeply into screw sizes, other than to say that wood screws come in gauges 1–14, and the most commonly used are gauges 6–10 from ½–2in (12–50mm). Generally, metric sizes in screws are not found, although one or two are just beginning to be used.

A selection of small screws for cabinet work

ABOVE From left to right: A Pozidriv screw head, a Phillips screw head and a slotted screw head.

PRACTICAL TIPS

• When screwing into hardwood, drill a pilot hole slightly smaller than the screw's diameter to ease the screw through.

• When fitting brass screws, first assemble the project with steel screws of the same gauge and length. Brass is very soft and the screws may shear off if used to cut their own threads.

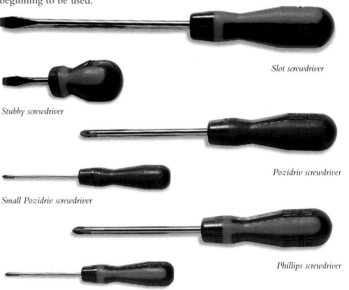

Slot screwdriver

Stubby screwdriver

Pozidriv screwdriver

Small Pozidriv screwdriver

Phillips screwdriver

Small Phillips screwdriver

SCREWDRIVER TYPES

For woodworking, the traditional hand screwdriver has an oval wooden handle and is used to drive slot-head screws only. This is widely available in a variety of sizes. A range of plastic-handled tools of various sizes are also available, designed to drive Phillips and Pozidriv screws, as well as slot-heads.

Power screwdrivers and drill/drivers vastly increase the rate of work. They can offer various torque settings that allow the screw heads to be set just flush with the work surface. Power drivers are also very useful for dismantling screwed joints and furniture because they will run in reverse.

Keeping the head of a slotted-screwdriver correctly ground to prevent it from slipping is very important. Remember also that the blade width must equal the length of the screw slot for the greatest

Cordless electric drill and screwdriver

A selection of drill bits

efficiency and to prevent both slipping and damage to the screw head. Always use the correct size of screwdriver with Phillips and Pozidriv screws, otherwise both the screw head and the screwdriver will be damaged.

USING SCREWS

Drilling a screw is a more skilled operation than nailing. It is usually advisable to drill pilot holes first to ease the screws' passage through the wood and to ensure that they go in straight. In hardwoods, pre-drilling is vital, otherwise the screws will just shear off when pressure is exerted by the screwdriver. Brass screws are particularly soft and need steel screws inserted before them (and then removed) to pre-cut the thread.

FAR LEFT Always drill pilot holes for brass hinge screws.

LEFT When fitting slot-head screws in a line, a neat finish can be achieved by setting all the heads so that they face the same way.

BELOW FAR LEFT Where possible, use the screwdriver with both hands to prevent slippage.

BELOW LEFT Screw holes should be marked very carefully when fitting hinges.

BELOW The correct way to bore and countersink when joining two planks of timber.

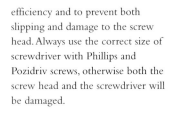

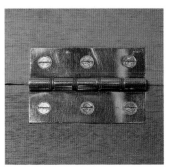

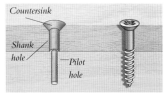

Countersink

Shank hole

Pilot hole

Saws

Sawing by hand and with power saws is a skill that must be learned well. Power saws do not take the skill out of sawing, or at least not all of it; they simply reduce the amount of hard work involved. You need to understand what types of saw are used for what purposes, and why, for the best results. There are dozens of special saws, but those covered here are all commonly used.

Hand saws

The most common saw in the home workshop is the hand saw. This is used for cross-cutting (across the grain) and ripping (along the grain), and the teeth of the saw are set accordingly, so you will need to ask your tool supplier for the correct one. There are also general-purpose hand saws that are reasonably suited to both tasks, and these are quite often hardpoint saws, which cannot be sharpened, but their specially hardened teeth give them a long life.

The tenon saw, sometimes called a backsaw, because of the solid strengthening bar along its top edge, is made specifically for cutting the tenons for making mortise-and-tenon joints and other fine work. Really fine work is done with a dovetail saw, which is similar to a tenon saw, but has more teeth to the inch to give a finer cut.

The tenon saw is often used with a bench hook for accurate cutting, and

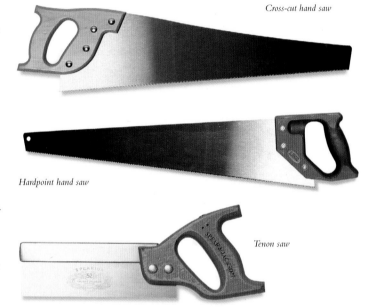

Cross-cut hand saw

Hardpoint hand saw

Tenon saw

one can be made quite easily as a do-it-yourself project. They usually measure about 300 x 150mm (12 x 6in). The mitre box is another handy aid for use with a tenon saw,

allowing 90- and 45-degree angles to be cut accurately, but the beginner is best advised to buy one rather than attempt to make one since accuracy is vital.

Mitre box

Bench hook

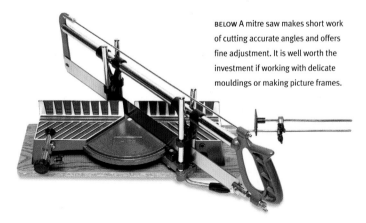

BELOW A mitre saw makes short work of cutting accurate angles and offers fine adjustment. It is well worth the investment if working with delicate mouldings or making picture frames.

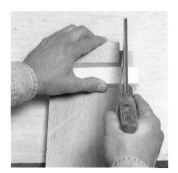

SAWING TECHNIQUES

When beginning a cut with a hand saw, draw the saw back toward your body to sever the wood fibres and produce a small kerf – the groove in which the saw blade will run. Always cut on the waste side of the marked line for perfect results.

When using a mitre box to make an angled cut, begin with the back of the saw raised slightly. This will make the cut easier to start. The bench hook also makes cross-cutting very easy at 90 degrees.

POWER TOOLS

A hand-held circular saw can be used for both cross-cutting and ripping, and many are supplied with a dual-purpose, tungsten-carbide-tipped blade for a long life. It is almost a necessity for the home woodworker and is an excellent investment; there are many quite inexpensive and reliable brands.

Another very handy tool is the jigsaw (saber saw). This comes into its own for cutting curves, but it can also save a lot of hard work when used to cut curved shapes from manufactured boards.

If a lot of curved or shaped work is envisaged, a small bandsaw is a useful addition to the workshop. These can be inexpensive.

Fret/scroll saws are very similar to jigsaws, having a reciprocating movement. They are used for fine pierced and detail work, and are capable of producing very delicate results. Most jigsaws come into their own when cutting manufactured boards, such as medium-density fibreboard, plywood or chipboard.

ABOVE LEFT Draw the saw back to start the cut.

ABOVE CENTRE Use a tenon saw for cutting small components or sawing tenons and the like. Point the nose of the saw downwards initially to start the cut.

ABOVE Use a bench hook for cross-cutting.

PRACTICAL TIPS

• Most cheap saws are not worth owning. Buy good ones, and hang them up or keep the blades guarded when they are not in use. Keep them dry, sharp, well set and lightly oiled.

• Always find a comfortable position to saw in. It will produce better results and reduce the risks of back strain or other injury.

FAR LEFT A circular saw will make light work of cutting timber, but be sure not to overload it, and always have the guards in place. Use a good-quality hand saw for smaller jobs.

LEFT A jigsaw (saber saw) is very good for cutting out curves and circles. Be sure your work is well clamped to keep it steady and firmly in place.

Nails, Hammers and Punches

There is no such thing as an "ordinary" nail. All nails have been derived for specific uses, although some can be put to several uses. Similarly, various types of hammer are available – always use the correct tool for the job. Wooden-handled hammers have a natural spring in the handles, which makes them easier to control than steel-handled ones.

Nails

The wire nail can be used for many simple tasks, such as box making, fencing and general carpentry, as can lost head and oval nails where there is no need for a flat head or when it is desirable for the nails to be concealed, such as when fixing cladding or boards. These wire nails can be considered as general-purpose fixings.

Oval wire nails can be driven below the surface of the work with less likelihood of them splitting the wood. They should be driven with their heads in line with the grain.

The cut nail is stamped from metal sheet and has a tapering, rectangular section, which gives it excellent holding properties. They are largely used for fixing flooring.

Panel pins (brads), as their name suggests, are used for fixing thin panels and cladding. They are nearly always punched out of sight below the surface, as are veneer pins.

When there is a need to secure thin or fragile sheet material, such as roofing felt or plasterboard (gypsum board), large-headed nails are used. These are commonly called clout nails, but may also be found under specific names, such as roofing nails and plasterboard nails. Their large heads spread the pressure and prevent the materials from tearing or crumbling. They are usually galvanized to protect against rust when used outdoors. Zinc nails are used for roofing because they are rustproof and easy to cut when renewing slates.

Dovetail nailing

When several nails are being driven into one piece of timber, avoid putting them in straight; slanting them will help prevent splitting.

Cross, or dovetail, nailing is a simple and useful method of holding a butt joint strongly in end grain.

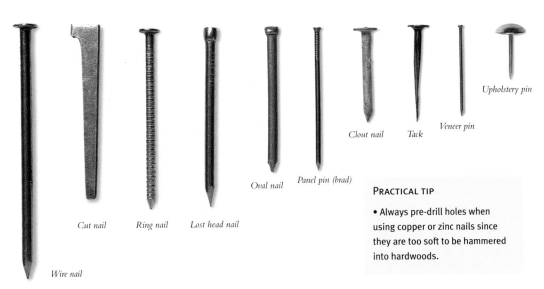

Upholstery pin

Clout nail   *Tack*   *Veneer pin*

Oval nail   *Panel pin (brad)*

Cut nail   *Ring nail*   *Lost head nail*

Wire nail

Practical tip

• Always pre-drill holes when using copper or zinc nails since they are too soft to be hammered into hardwoods.

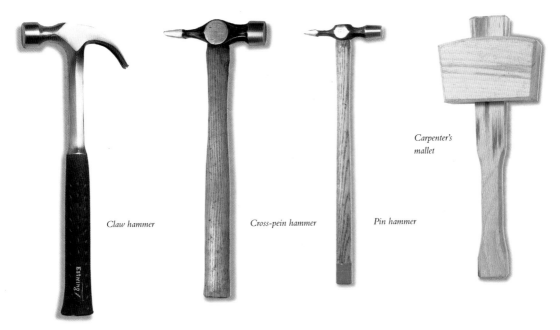

Claw hammer *Cross-pein hammer* *Pin hammer* *Carpenter's mallet*

HAMMERS

The most essential hammer for the woodworker is the claw hammer. About 365–450g (13–16oz) is a good weight to aim for, since the hammer should be heavy enough to drive fairly large nails. It is a mistake to use a hammer that is too light, as this tends to bend the nails rather than drive them.

For lighter nails, a cross-pein or Warrington hammer is useful, since the flat head can be used to start the nail or pin without risk of hitting your fingers. For even smaller panel pins (brads), the pin hammer is used.

THE MALLET

It should be remembered that the carpenter's mallet, often made from solid beech, is a form of hammer, but it should never be used for striking anything other than wood or similar soft materials or serious damage will result.

REMOVING AND HIDING NAILS

Nails or pins can be removed from a workpiece by using a specialized tool such as a nail puller. You might need to use this if you have bent the nail or perhaps if you are working with previously-used timber. Alternatively, the claw of a claw hammer can be easily employed.

Very often, we need to punch nail heads below the surface of the work and fill the resulting small holes with a wood filler. Nail sets are used for this, and they come in various sizes. Each has a very slightly concave tip to cover the nail head and prevent slipping. Nail sets should not be confused with centre punches, which are used to mark metal for drilling.

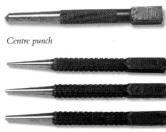

Centre punch

Nail sets or punches

Nail puller

ABOVE The claw hammer's ability to extract, as well as drive, nails makes it a useful tool for the carpentry shop.

SANDERS

Although the term "sanding" is generally used for do-it-yourself projects, it is something of a misnomer. A truer description would be "abrading", because what we call "sandpaper" is, in fact, "glasspaper". In addition, we also use garnet paper, and silicon-carbide and aluminium-oxide abrasive papers, all of which shape wood very efficiently.

GRIT SIZE

One thing abrasive papers all have in common is classification by grit size, and the golden rule is to work progressively down through the grit sizes, from coarse to fine, when smoothing a piece of work. For example, 400 grit is finer than 200 grit and should be employed later in the finishing process. Abrasives can be used by hand or with a variety of machines, both hand-held and stationary. Sanders are also suitable for shaping work, using coarse abrasives for rapid material removal.

TYPES OF SANDER

A tool commonly used for heavy-duty shaping and sanding is the belt sander. These normally have a 75mm (3in) wide belt, running continuously over two rollers and a dust collection facility in the form of a cloth bag.

Most home craftsmen are likely to own an orbital sander, which is useful for general light sanding work such as finishing boards. These sanders are designed to accept either half or a third of a standard-size abrasive sheet and quite often have dedicated sheets made for them. Random orbital sanders are similar, but often employ self-adhesive abrasive sheets that are easy to fit. They can be small enough to be used with one hand in tight spots, but still give a good finish to most types of work. A newcomer to the sanding armoury is the power abrader. This tool can remove material rapidly and should be regarded as a shaping or sculptural tool rather than a pure sander.

PRACTICAL TIPS

• Most clogged-up sanding discs and belts can be cleaned by pressing a piece of plastic pipe, such as garden hose, on to the belt with the motor running.

• Always finish off your sanding by hand, working along the grain of the wood.

Belt sander

Orbital sander

Random orbital sander

Palm orbital sander

Detail sander

LEFT AND ABOVE Power sanders are most useful for the quick removal of waste stock before finishing by hand. A belt sander is worth considering if you have a lot of heavy-duty work, but does not produce an acceptable finish on its own. For general use, an orbital sander is by far the most versatile power tool to buy.

Hand sanding

This is used to finish fine cabinet work. Always work along the grain of the wood. Use a cork or rubber block on flat surfaces to obtain the right amount of flexibility that you will need. Clear the dust away as you work to avoid clogging the paper, particularly on resinous and oily wood. To finish off a rounded edge, wrap a square of paper around a section of moulded timber with the correct profile for the job.

Static sanders

Very inexpensive and well worth owning is the combination sander. This consists of a belt and disc sander combined and is invaluable in the home workshop. Static sanders are almost exclusively shaping and trimming tools, rather than smoothers, since the workpiece is taken to them. Many have mitre fences for multi-angled cutting, and worktables that can be adjusted to exactly 90 degrees for the work in hand. They can be very aggressive unless handled with care.

Making a sanding block

1 Fold your sheet of abrasive paper to size and tear it along a sharp edge.

2 Wrap the abrasive around a cork block or similar soft material before starting to sand.

ABOVE Dedicated belt and disc sanders are now reasonably priced and they are very useful tools in the home workshop.

ABOVE The belt sander can be inverted and secured in a woodworking vice. Use the rounded ends of the belt to shape concave curves.

ABOVE The fast action of the belt sander means that it must be held with both hands to prevent it from running away.

ABOVE The orbital sander is a much less ferocious cutter than the belt sander and is easy to control. They are sold as half-sheet, third-sheet and quarter-sheet models. Standard-sized paper fits the base.

ABOVE The power abrader has many uses, one of which is as a sculptural tool for shaping different kinds of wood.

PLANES

Unplaned wood is known as "sawn" and comes in sizes such as 50 x 25mm (2 x 1in) or 100 x 50mm (4 x 2in). In spite of the ready availability of prepared (planed/dressed) timber, the do-it-yourself enthusiast must still learn to use at least one hand plane in the pursuit of this craft – for trimming joints and joining faces, and for the general cleaning up of timber surfaces.

USING PLANES

By using a hand plane to remove wood, a beginner will gain a better understanding of the characteristics of the wood being worked. The most commonly used variety is the small jack, or smoothing plane.

Good-quality examples are sufficiently weighty to avoid "chatter", which occurs when the plane skips over the surface of the wood without cutting properly.

Shoulder plane

Jack plane

Smoothing plane

Shoulder plane

Block plane

HAND PLANING TECHNIQUES

Body weight plays a large part in planing technique. Position your body with your hips and shoulders in line with the plane, and your feet spaced comfortably apart.

At the beginning of the stroke, apply pressure to the front handle of the plane, switching to a general downward pressure during the middle of the stroke, and finish off by applying most of the pressure to the back of the plane at the end of the board.

STARTING TO PLANE

1 The correct body position helps to achieve the desired result.

2 Keep the pressure on the back of the plane at the end of your stroke.

PRACTICAL TIPS

• Cheap planes often serve to blunt enthusiasm by poor performance. Always buy the best you can afford and keep them sharp.

• Check for sharpness and adjustment each time a plane is used – and make sure the wood to be planed is held firmly.

3 To keep the plane centralized, tuck your fingers under the sole plate as a guide.

4 If you have identical edges to plane, clamp them together and work on both at once.

Planing end grain and boards

A block plane is often used for planing end grain because its blade is set at a low angle that severs the wood fibres cleanly. To avoid splitting the ends of the wood, work in from each side toward the middle.

A useful technique for planing wide boards is to work diagonally, or even at right angles, across the grain of the boards. This method will remove material efficiently. To finish, it will be necessary to make cuts with the grain for a smooth surface.

Chamfer cutting

This is often a quick operation, but it is easy to get carried away. So, for accuracy, always mark the extent of the desired chamfer with a pencil or marking knife before planing.

The electric planer

Electric planers can be aggressive when removing stock, so hold the tool with both hands and keep it moving so that it does not cut for too long in one spot. An electric planer can also be used across the grain of wide boards for quick results, provided final finishing is with the grain. Although the electric planer is very fast, the hand-held version rarely gives the quality of finish that can be achieved with a well-set and sharpened bench plane.

Sharpening plane irons

Apply a coat of thin oil to the oilstone and rest the bevel of the iron on the stone. Hold the blade at 35 degrees to the oilstone and maintain a constant angle while working it backward and forward on the stone. Honing jigs, which set the angle exactly, are readily available, but most craftsmen soon learn to do this accurately by hand. Lay the back of the iron flat on the oilstone and slowly rub off the burr formed by the sharpening process. Clean any debris from inside the body of the plane before reassembly, and apply a drop of oil to the moving parts of the adjustment mechanism.

Making chamfers

1 Mark out a chamfer to ensure an even removal of the material.

2 Plane a chamfer by hand with a firm grip and tool control.

1 Keep the block at a steady angle along the sharpening stone.

Planing

ABOVE Use two hands to plane end grain with an electric planer to ensure complete control.

ABOVE Plane across wide boards with an electric planer to give quick results.

2 Remove the burr or "back off" from a newly sharpened blade.

KNIVES

When we think of knives in relation to woodworking, the most common application is the marking or striking knife. However, the do-it-yourself enthusiast will need a variety of other knives, some of which have very specific functions. Some do not actually conform to the conventional idea of a knife at all, but all have metal blades and are essentially cutting tools.

MARKING KNIVES

The purpose of a marking knife is to mark a sawing line by lightly cutting the surface wood fibres and assist in the beginning of a sawcut. Not only does this provide a permanent guide line, but it also prevents the fibres from splintering as the saw cuts through. These tools are usually about 200mm (8in) and make a much finer line than a pencil.

They are normally used in conjunction with a steel rule, straightedge or square and are bevelled on one side only so that they can be used tight against the steel edge for accuracy. They are available in both left- and right-handed versions.

Marking knives without pointed ends are also frequently used, and these are bevelled on either the left- or right-hand side, depending on the needs of the user.

Twin-bladed knives are available and are adjusted by a set screw and locking knob. Typically, the blades can be set to a spacing of 3–19mm (⅛–¾in). This type of knife is used for marking parallel lines, gauging mortises and cutting thin strips from veneers for inlay work.

ABOVE Mark a line across the grain with the knife held firmly against the steel edge of a try square. This gives a very fine line of severed wood fibres, which is ideal to work to with either a saw or a chisel.

MARKING OUT

A typical example of a marking knife being used in conjunction with a steel rule. Note how the fingers of the hand are spread to keep a firm and even downward pressure on the rule, allowing the knife to be used hard against the rule's edge.

Striking knife with blade and point

Marking knife with bevel on one side

Twin-bladed adjustable marking knife

Heavy-duty retractable blade knife

GENERAL-PURPOSE KNIVES

By far the most common and useful general-purpose knife is the craft, or "Stanley" knife, that stores replacement blades in the handle. This is an indispensable tool in any workshop, and it can be used for many purposes, including marking out.

Another very handy tool in the workshop is the scalpel. More delicate and invasive than the craft knife, a scalpel is ideal for cutting out templates and particularly useful for cleaning up deeply indented cuts in carvings and routed work. Scalpels are made with a variety of handles and have replaceable blades.

MISCELLANEOUS KNIVES

Putty knives often find their way into the do-it-yourself enthusiast's tool kit. They have specially shaped ends to their blades to make "cutting off" easier. This means withdrawing the knife from the work without damaging the soft putty that is being applied to a window pane or moulding for example.

The filling knife is a familiar decorator's tool with a flexible spring-tempered blade that is ideal for forcing soft material, such as wood filler, into knot holes, cracks and blemishes in timber, and plaster filler into cracks in walls. These

PRACTICAL TIPS

• Never use a scalpel or craft knife with excessive pressure. The blade may snap off and pieces fly up into your unprotected eyes.

• Always place the hand not holding the knife behind the blade of a trimming knife. This prevents injury if the blade slips.

come in a variety of shapes and sizes and are often confused with stripping knives, which have thicker and less flexible blades.

Craft knife with replaceable blades

Putty knives (above and below)

Lightweight craft knife with a choice of blades

A decorator's knife

Wide stripping knife

A selection of scalpels

Narrow stripping knife

Tackers

Staple guns, or tackers, have a wide variety of uses around the home and are particularly useful when working alone. They can quickly secure light materials in position for fixing with nails or screws later. Moreover, they can be used one-handed, allowing the other hand to stretch and position the material for fixing, which can often produce more accurate results.

Fixing sheet materials and cables

Tackers come into their own for fixing virtually any sheet material, either to solid timber or manufactured boards such as chipboard, plywood and blockboard. The more powerful models are capable of fixing into plaster and soft masonry. A tacker is an essential item for upholstery work, ideal for fitting hardboard to floors and securing carpet underlay, as well as fixing roofing felt and ceiling tiles, and it can even be used to secure low-voltage electrical cables such as those used for door bells. Few are recommended for attaching cables carrying mains electricity, but special wiring tackers can be bought that will fire U-shaped staples for fixing cables up to 6mm (¼in) diameter.

Tacker types

Many tackers are similar to the hand-operated staplers found in every office. Electrically powered tools, for either light or heavy duty, pack a real punch. Those operated by compressed air are generally for heavy-duty use and are ideal for jobs such as fixing wire mesh, netting and heavy sheeting.

Many tackers will operate with either staples or nails and some are dedicated nailers only. The latter may fire up to 30 nails per minute.

Picture framers use smaller dedicated tools that fire special flexible points into the frame to hold both the glass and the backing. Some have an adjustable power control to match the hardness of the timber, as

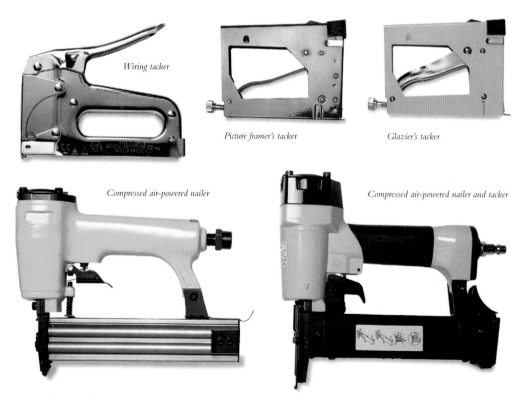

Wiring tacker

Picture framer's tacker

Glazier's tacker

Compressed air-powered nailer

Compressed air-powered nailer and tacker

do many of the more expensive general-purpose tackers.

Glaziers use a frame tool that fires brads up to 19mm (¾in) long to secure the glass in a window frame. It leaves the heads projecting about 4mm (¾₆in) before glazing with putty. A more general application of this tool is for temporary fixings where the projecting head makes the brad or panel pin easy to remove.

GENERAL-PURPOSE TACKERS

A hand-operated, heavy-duty staple gun is worked by gripping the body and squeezing down with the handle. Many have a small window that allows the contents of the magazine to be checked. A heavy-duty electronic tacker machine fires

single staples, nails or pins and will accept staple widths of 4 and 10mm (¾₆ and ⅜in) with lengths up to 23mm (⅞in). It also takes nails and pins up to 23mm (⅞in) long. It is ideal for fixing tongued-and-grooved cladding and heavy sheeting such as hardboard.

A typical nailer/tacker multiple-impact tool with electronic adjustment is ideal for upholstery work and general fixing around the home. Single-shot, continuous tacking or tacking two staples at a time can be achieved with this general-purpose tool.

Used in much the same way as a hammer, a hammer tacker feeds and drives staples as fast as the operator can use it. More suited to speed than

accuracy, it earns its keep when something needs fixing in place quickly or if the finished result is not visually important.

PRACTICAL TIPS

• Never point a nail gun or powered tacker at anybody. New tools have safety devices to prevent operation when not in contact with the workpiece, but it is not worth taking chances, especially with an older tool.

• Always buy a brand of tacker that uses a standard size of nail or staple, making sure these are available locally.

Hammer tacker

Electronic staple gun

Hand-operated, heavy-duty staple gun

Stapler/nail gun

Clamps

Many do-it-yourself tasks require two or more sections of a workpiece to be held together temporarily while a more permanent fixing is made, often with glue. A variety of clamps is available for this purpose, many of them with specific uses. Keen woodworkers may make their own clamps (or cramps as they are often called) from scrap wood or other materials.

Commonly used clamps

The most common clamp in the workshop is the G-clamp. This is a general-purpose tool that is available with a variety of throat sizes. It may be used on its own or in conjunction with others when, for example, working on the surface of a wide board or holding boards together for gluing.

The sash clamp was specifically designed for assembling window frames, or sashes, but it is also often used when edge-jointing boards to form large panels for table tops and similar items.

Sometimes, it is useful to be able to apply a clamp with one hand while holding the workpiece in the other, which is when the single-handed clamp comes into its own. It works on a simple ratchet system, rather like a mastic (caulking) gun.

For picture framing and heavier items with 45-degree mitres at the corners, there is the mitre clamp. This can be quite a complex affair with screw handles or a very simple clothes-peg (pin) type arrangement, that is applied very quickly.

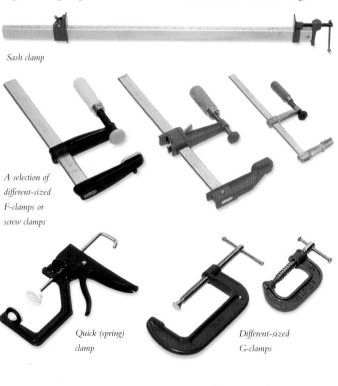

Sash clamp

A selection of different-sized F-clamps or screw clamps

Quick (spring) clamp

Different-sized G-clamps

Web clamp

Mitre clamp

ABOVE Small wooden picture frames and mirrors can be easily joined with inexpensive mitre clamps.

ABOVE This clever little clamp works on spring pressure and can be applied quickly.

Special-purpose clamps

There are many of these, but one that the do-it-yourself enthusiast may find useful is the cam clamp, which is wooden with cork faces. This is a quickly operated clamp often used by musical instrument makers. Its advantages are its speed in use, its lightness and its simplicity. The cam clamp is ideal for small holding jobs around the home, although it cannot exert a great deal of pressure.

Another useful standby is the web, frame or strap clamp. This is perfect for holding unusually-shaped items,

Cam clamp

which can be pulled together from a single point.

They are most commonly used to join coopered work, such as barrels and casks, or multi-faceted shapes such as hexagons or octagons used in decorative frames and mirrors. The components to be joined usually lie flat on a horizontal surface, as shown.

ABOVE The web or strap clamp is ideal for multi-sided shapes that are difficult to hold. The strong nylon webbing extends around the work and is tightened with a spanner, applying tension equally around the work.

Clamps in use

Apply pressure to a joint or the assembly you are working on as soon as possible after gluing – make a habit of preparing everything you need in advance. Keep a box of small scraps of wood handy and use them to protect the surface of the work. It is often said that you can never have too many clamps, and you will soon start collecting a selection of different types and sizes to suit all kinds of assembly technique. Many of these you can make yourself.

ABOVE Use sash clamps to edge-joint boards to form a panel such as a table top. Reverse the central clamp to even out the pressure.

ABOVE Home-made clamps used for the same purpose, but this time the pressure is exerted by means of wedges.

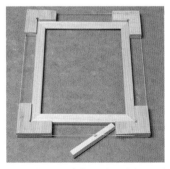

ABOVE A home-made frame clamp being used on a picture frame. There are grooved blocks at the corners to hold the string.

ABOVE The G-clamp in a typical application. Note the packing pieces beneath the jaws to prevent bruising of the wood.

Practical tips

• Do not be tempted to release clamps too quickly. Be patient, allowing plenty of drying time for the glue.

• Think through the sequence for the clamping process and make sure you have enough clamps to hand before you apply any glue. You may decide you need another person to help.

WORKBENCHES AND VICES

A solid and stable surface is essential for producing good work, and serious thought should be given to this by the enthusiast. A good bench need not be too expensive, nor too pretty; the prime requirements are sturdy construction, a flat top surface and at least one good vice somewhere on the front of the bench.

WORKBENCHES

A basic bench with a front vice can be improved by the addition of a tail vice and bench dogs. The bench can be improved still further by incorporating a cabinet and drawers. The bench dogs are set at a convenient length into a series of holes in the top of the bench and they work in conjunction with the tail vice for holding long pieces of timber along the top of the bench. They can easily be removed and reset at will.

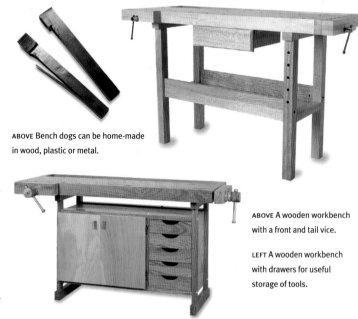

ABOVE Bench dogs can be home-made in wood, plastic or metal.

ABOVE A wooden workbench with a front and tail vice.

LEFT A wooden workbench with drawers for useful storage of tools.

PORTABLE SUPPORTS

By far the most popular form of portable support is the foldaway workbench. This is really convenient to use, both in the workshop and the home, both internally and externally. It has the ingenious feature of a bench top that is in two halves and is capable of acting as a vice. It is handy for holding awkward shapes, such as pipes and large dowels.

Another form of a simple, portable bench is the saw horse, or trestle. A pair of these will support large workpieces such as doors. It is an ideal first-time project for a do-it-yourself enthusiast to make, providing experience in cutting angles and simple jointwork.

ABOVE A portable foldaway workbench with adjustable bench top.

ABOVE Wooden sawhorses come in pairs and are often home-made.

ABOVE Plastic, light-weight sawhorses can be useful if you are undertaking small jobs.

VICES

Your main workshop vice should be heavy and sturdy. It is normally screwed to the underside of the work bench or worktop, close to one of the legs. Make sure you buy one that is designed for woodworking, preferably with a quick-release action on the front of the vice that allows you to open and close the jaws quickly, turning the handle for final adjustments. You should certainly be able to fit false wooden jaws to prevent bruising of the work.

Additional ways of protecting the work in the vice take the form of magnetic vice jaws faced with cork, rubber or aluminium, which fit inside the main jaws of the steel bench vice.

Another useful, portable, addition to the bench that is cheaper than a woodworking vice is the swivelling bench-top vice. This can easily be fitted and removed very quickly, usually by means of a screw clamp. It is particularly handy for holding down small pieces of work in awkward positions, when carving for example. However, it is too lightweight to hold work that is to be struck hard.

The mitre clamp can also be considered as a bench vice of sorts and is useful to picture framers. Most woodworkers will keep one near the bench to hold any assemblies that require clamping at 45 degrees. Good quality ones are made from metal, since plastic will tend to flex when pressure is applied.

RIGHT A solid carpenter's vice is an absolute essential tool in the workshop, second only to the workbench itself.

ABOVE A swivelling bench-top vice is handy for work that needs to be turned or that is an awkward shape to work.

ABOVE False faces for vices come in rubber, cork and aluminium and prevent damage to the wood being worked.

ABOVE A picture framer's vice is best made from metal rather than plastic.

PRACTICAL TIPS

• Always buy the best-quality vice you can afford; second-hand ones can be particularly good value.

• Spend time adjusting your workbench to the exact height that suits you. An incorrect height can prove to be very tiring and is not good for your back. Never shorten the legs of a bench if it is too high; work off a duckboard if necessary.

FOLDING BENCH VICE

The worktop acts as two vice jaws, one of which can be slewed to grip tapered items of work or straightened up to fit parallel-sided wood using the vice controls at the side of the bench. On some makes, the adjustable jaw can also be set vertically to provide downward clamping pressure. You can also clamp a piece of wood to the top of the bench between the plastic clamping pegs to hold awkwardly shaped pieces.

Put the piece of wood or other item you wish to saw between the vice jaws.

PINCERS AND PLIERS

Every do-it-yourself enthusiast's tool kit should include a range of hand tools for gripping small items. Chief among these are pincers, used for removing nails and similar fixings, and general-purpose combination pliers, which offer a variety of gripping and cutting features. Many other special-purpose tools of similar design are also available.

REMOVING NAILS AND TACKS

A good pair of pincers will remove nails and tacks with little trouble. The rolling action required to remove a nail with pincers is very similar to that used with a claw hammer. Pincers are essential to the woodworker, an ideal length is about 175mm (7in) to ensure good leverage. The jaws should touch along their entire width and be properly aligned to provide maximum grip.

It is important that pincers have good leverage and do not damage the work, and for this reason, broad jaws – about 25mm (1in) wide – that will spread the load are best.

Some pincers come with a handy tack lifter on one of the handles. Purpose-made tack lifters are very useful for upholstery work, and if you intend doing any furniture making or restoration, it is well worth investing in one.

Another special tack and nail remover is the nail puller, or "cat's-paw", as it is sometimes known. This tool has a standard tack remover at one end and a large, right-angled claw at the other for getting under the heads of stubborn nails. The claw can be tapped under the head of an embedded nail with a small hammer.

LEFT The flat behind the claw of this Japanese nail puller can be tapped with a hammer to drive the claw under the nail head.

REUSING NAILS AND WOOD

When removing an old nail from better-quality wood that is to be reused, protect the surface of the wood by slipping a piece of hardboard or thin plywood below the pincer head.

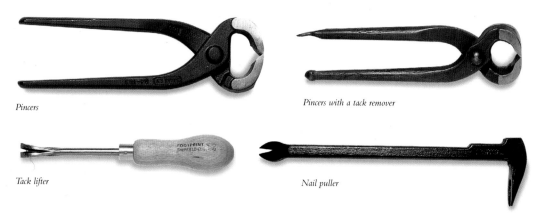

Pincers

Pincers with a tack remover

Tack lifter

Nail puller

PLIERS

These come in a bewildering range of types and sizes, many of which have very specific uses.

Combination pliers are "Jacks of all trades" and are used for gripping, twisting and cutting. They come in various sizes, but a good pair would be about 200mm (8in) long and probably have plastic or rubber handle grips for comfort and insulation against shock.

LONG-NOSED (NEEDLENOSE) PLIERS

These are rather more specialized and are used for gripping small objects in confined spaces. Some have cranked jaws at various angles for access to awkward places. They come in many sizes and some are designed for very fine work.

SPECIALIZED GRIPPING AND CUTTING TOOLS

Glass pliers are used for gripping and shaping glass and ceramic tiles. They are usually made with bare steel handles to prevent any sharp particles from sticking to them.

Long-nosed, vice-grip pliers will hold very small objects in awkward spots and are useful for extracting small items embedded in wood.

Standard vice-grips are familiar to generations of craftspeople. They provide a powerful grip to hold all manner of objects in a variety of materials. Because they have locking handles, they can be very useful as miniature vices when gluing up small objects. Power cutters are less well known, but have razor-sharp replaceable blades for cutting sheet

materials such as plastics and thin metals. They are handy in the workshop for making patterns and cutting templates.

HOLDING PLIERS

When using pliers, hold them firmly, keeping your palm away from the pivot, which can pinch your skin as the jaws close.

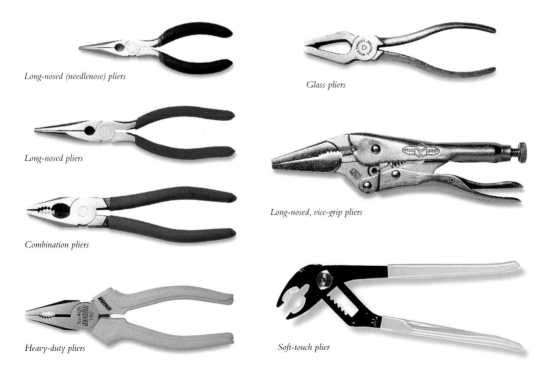

Long-nosed (needlenose) pliers

Glass pliers

Long-nosed pliers

Combination pliers

Long-nosed, vice-grip pliers

Heavy-duty pliers

Soft-touch plier

Spanners and Wrenches

Although spanners and wrenches may be thought of as tools for the garage, there are many do-it-yourself tasks that require these gripping and twisting tools, particularly in the kitchen and bathroom, where you are likely to come into contact with pipes and their fittings. All home workshops need at least one comprehensive set of sockets or spanners.

Spanners

These are necessary in the home workshop where power tools and machinery are involved. They are needed for changing the blades on circular saws, for adjusting and setting bandsaw guides, and for assembling all manner of machinery stands, tool racks and benches. You should have a selection of wrenches and spanners in the home workshop. The combination spanner, open-ended spanner and the ring spanner are usually purchased in sets; the other tools are bought singly.

There is a large range to choose from, and it is essential to use a spanner that fits a nut or bolt perfectly, otherwise the fixing will be damaged and the user runs the risk of skinned knuckles. Spanners are graduated in specific sizes – metric, Whitworth and A/F are the most common. Open-ended spanners are the most usual. Some have jaws that are offset by about 15 degrees to allow them to get on to different flats of nuts when working in tight spots.

Ring spanners have enclosed heads that give a more secure grip. They may have six or 12 points and can be used on square or hexagonal nuts and bolts. The 12-point version needs only a very small movement for it to contact new flats on the nut or bolt head, so is very useful where there is limited room for movement.

ABOVE Socket sets are extremely useful in any home workshop and offer the owner a choice of types of drives (such as bars or ratchets) as well as sockets in a variety of sizes.

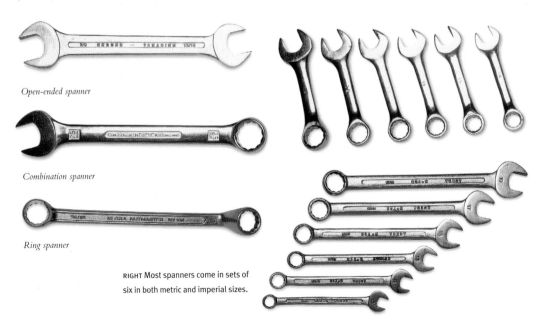

Open-ended spanner

Combination spanner

Ring spanner

RIGHT Most spanners come in sets of six in both metric and imperial sizes.

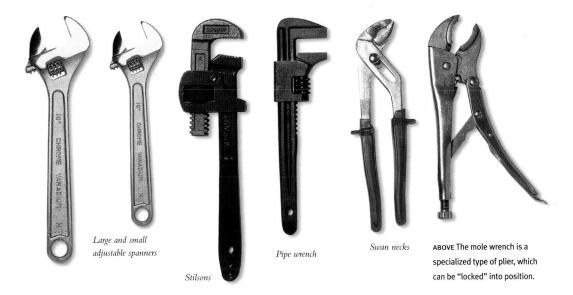

Large and small adjustable spanners

Stilsons

Pipe wrench

Swan necks

ABOVE The mole wrench is a specialized type of plier, which can be "locked" into position.

Sockets grip in the same manner as a ring spanner, but are designed to fit a variety of drive handles, of which the ratchet handle is the most useful. This enables the user to continue to turn a nut or bolt without having to remove the socket after each turn. Some large sets offer metric, Whitworth, BSF and A/F sizes. Small sets of additional sockets are available to complement your existing set, allowing you to build up a kit that meets your needs exactly.

The auto-adjustable wrench is quick and easy to use. Normally, the adjustable spanner is made from forged alloy steel. Self-grip wrenches, or vice grips, can be adjusted to fit pipework or on a nut or bolt head, and can then be locked to grip tightly. They are very versatile and useful tools. Water-pump pliers offer five or six settings by virtue of having an adjustable bottom jaw. They exert a heavy pressure because of their long handles.

ABOVE Allen keys are specially made for using with screws that have corresponding hexagonal holes in their heads.

WRENCHES
Adjustable spanners and wrenches enable the user to grip various sizes and types of fittings. Some are designed for specific purposes, while others are suitable for more general household use.

Basic plumbing tools include adjustable pipe wrenches (known as Stilsons), an adjustable basin wrench, a double-ended basin wrench and water-pump pliers with soft jaws.

ABOVE These soft pliable grips, called "boa wrenches", can be used successfully on awkwardly shaped work, such as for opening containers or use them on polished surfaces.

PRACTICAL TIP

• Never use a wrench on a nut or bolt if a spanner of the correct size is available. Wrenches are essentially for pipe work and will damage the corners of nuts and bolt heads very quickly. Use the correct tool wherever possible.

CHISELS

These come in a variety of shapes and sizes, all with specific uses. For jobs around the home, only three basic types are required. Most commonly used is the firmer chisel, which is a compromise between a mortise chisel and a bevel-edged chisel. It can be regarded as a general-purpose tool and has a strong blade of rectangular section designed for medium–heavy work.

SPECIAL-PURPOSE CHISELS

Bevel-edged and paring chisels have thinner blades than firmer chisels. The tops of the blades are bevelled along their length to allow better access into small recesses and corners, and to permit fine slicing cuts to be made in the wood.

The mortise chisel is a sturdy tool with a lot of steel just below the handle. It is used for chopping deep mortises across the grain so has to be able to withstand blows from a heavy mallet without damage. For this reason, a wooden-handled mortise chisel may have a metal band around the top of the handle to prevent it from splitting. The thickness of the steel blade also allows it to be used as a lever for cleaning the waste from the mortise. Many new chisels have shatter-resistant polypropylene handles that can be struck with a mallet, or even a hammer, without damage since the handles are virtually unbreakable. However, use a thin-bladed paring chisel with hand pressure only.

LEFT A selection of the many chisels available. A small selection will cover most needs. Keep them sharp and guarded when not in use. Always keep your hands behind the cutting edge. Only hit them with a wooden mallet if they are wooden handled. A hammer can be used on heavy plastic-handled varieties of chisel. Bevel-edged chisels are the most versatile type you can buy for most tasks. A firmer chisel has a stronger blade designed to accept heavier blows.

PRACTICAL TIPS

• Always make sure your chisel is really sharp. A blunt tool needs more pressure to force it through the work and is more likely to slip, possibly causing an accident.

• Do not leave chisels lying on the bench where the blades can come into contact with metal objects. Hang them up, fit them with plastic blade guards, or keep them in a cloth or leather chisel roll like the professionals.

BLADE WIDTHS

These usually range from 3 to 25mm (⅛in to 1in) in graduations of 3mm. After 25mm, it is usual for the graduations to increase by 6mm (¼in). Most home woodworkers will find 6mm (¼in), 12mm (½in), 19mm (¾in) and 25mm (1in) sufficient for their needs.

Firmer chisel

Mortise chisel

Bevel-edged chisel

Plastic-handled chisels such as this may be struck with a mallet or a hammer

CHISELLING TECHNIQUES

Always aim to remove as much excess wood as possible from the cut before using the chisel. For example, remove the wood with a saw before cleaning up with a chisel or, when cutting a mortise, drill out as much of the waste as possible and use the chisel to clean and square-up the sides to take the tenon.

When using a router to cut slots and rebates, square off the ends with a chisel by hand.

Remember to cut away from the marked line when chiselling so that any splitting will occur in the waste wood, and always cut away from yourself to avoid injury. Work patiently and never be tempted to make cuts that are too large. The chisel should be pushed or struck with one hand while being guided with the other. Paring with a chisel is a skilled and satisfying task, but a really sharp tool is essential. A blunt chisel can slip and cause a lot of damage as soon as it loses its edge.

ABOVE Remove the bulk of the waste from a dovetail with a saw before chiselling.

ABOVE To form a mortise, remove most of the waste with a drill, then finish with a chisel.

ABOVE Vertical paring by hand, and with a mallet, needs both hands for total control.

ABOVE Hold the chisel vertically and strike firmly with the wooden mallet.

PARING

1 Horizontal paring, working from both sides to the middle, prevents "break out" and results in clean work using less pressure.

2 To chamfer an edge, first use the chisel with the bevel down, then make the finishing cuts bevel up by making fine cuts.

3 When you are making the finishing cuts bevel up, note how the thumb controls the cutting edge of the chisel, close to the work.

Toolboxes and Tool Storage

Tidy and effective storage in the workshop pays off in many ways. Properly stored tools are protected from the atmosphere and will not rust or discolour. The sharp, cutting edges of saws and chisels are prevented from damage, as are the potential user's fingers, and tools can always be easily found near at hand when they are needed.

STORAGE

Efficient storage saves bench and floor space for other uses, and tools are more easily located, saving time and frustration. It is well worth taking the trouble to devise, and even make your own storage facilities. There are plenty of benches, cabinets, racks, clips and tool rolls on the market so that you can equip your workshop with exactly what you need. Remember, too, that storage for tools often needs to be portable, so tool pouches and carrying bags also need to be part of the overall picture.

PORTABLE STORAGE

The traditional carpenter's tool bag can still be obtained. Made from heavy canvas, it has two carrying handles and brass eyelets for closing.

Compact, compartmentalized plastic or metal toolboxes with drawers, carrying handles and safety locks are another option for carrying tools from one job to another.

A leather tool pouch can be worn around the waist and has loops and pockets for tools as well as screws and nails. Various sizes and styles are available. They are ideal for use on projects that require you to keep moving about.

Drill bits and chisels should always be carried in a tool roll with their tips covered for protection. Many saws are sold with a plastic snap-on blade guard to protect the teeth when not in use.

TOP RIGHT A carpenter's canvas toolbag.

RIGHT A tool pouch worn around the waist is very helpful when working in different parts of the home.

Engineer's toolbox

Bit roll

Removeable trays are very handy

Plastic toolbox with separate compartments

Static storage

The most important static storage space is that below the workbench top, and often this takes the form of cabinets or drawers. A useful device is the large tilting drawer, which can easily be made and is ideal for storing tools that are in frequent use, such as planes and chisels.

Wall-mounted cabinets with sliding doors are really practical in the workshop. The sliding doors allow them to be sited in confined areas and make it impossible to hit your head on them when they are open, which is especially important above the workbench. Fitted with a few pegs, shelves and compartments, they can be very useful.

Shelving units come in a variety of materials, shapes and sizes, and most proprietary brands can be added to as the need arises.

The tool board has the great advantage of not only displaying the tools, but also making it immediately obvious when a tool has not been replaced. To make a simple version, arrange the tools you wish to store on a flat board and draw around them with a felt-tipped pen or black marker pen. Then fit suitable hooks, pegs or clips needed to hold them in place.

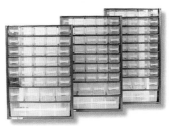

TOP AND ABOVE Specifically made in transparent plastics for easy identification of the contents, storage drawers for screws, nails, clips and a host of other small items are a must. They are best fitted to a wall at eye level, within reach of the bench.

ABOVE Make a home-made storage unit to keep your workshop drill bits tidy and easily accessible.

Tool boards

When making a tool board remember to leave space around each tool so that it can be lifted clear when the board is on the wall. The main drawback with tool boards is that they are usually in the open, which makes the tools prone to rust or theft.

ABOVE To make your own tool board, draw around the tools with a felt-tipped pen to indicate where they go. Hammer in nails or hooks that will hold them in place. Wall hooks will hold larger items, such as saws.

ABOVE Alternatively, you can buy a tool board made from plywood with holes from local builder's merchants. Insert spring clips that are widely available on the front of the tool board. These can also be fitted to the fronts of shelves.

Practical tips

• You can make a quick saw guard by simply cutting a slit along a length of garden hose and sliding it over the teeth of the saw blade.

• When not in a carrying roll, twist drills can be stored in a block close to the workbench or drill stand.

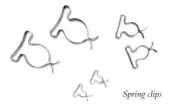

Spring clips

EQUIPMENT AND MATERIALS

In the same way that many modern tools are designed specifically with the do-it-yourself enthusiast in mind, much of the equipment and many of the materials used around the home have been developed for amateur use. Sometimes, of course, you will have no choice but to use the traditional equipment and materials, but today even these are more user-friendly.

Plaster

In traditionally-built houses made of bricks and blocks, the purpose of plaster is to provide smooth wall surfaces. It is applied to the inner surfaces of the masonry walls that form the outer shell of the building and to both sides of any internal masonry walls. Plastering is a skill acquired only with a lot of practice. Do-it-yourself plasters make the job easier.

Using plaster

Most plaster used inside houses is based on lightweight gypsum; cement-based plasters (often referred to as renders) are used for finishing the outside of walls, but may be used for renovation work inside where there is a damp problem.

The main types of plaster

Conventional lightweight gypsum plaster is applied in two coats: undercoat around 10mm (⅜in) thick in two layers, and finish coat about 3mm (⅛in) thick in a single layer. If the surface you are working on is particularly absorbent, choose an HSB (high-suction background) version of the undercoat plaster; similarly, special undercoat plasters are made for dense, less absorbent surfaces. You may also find finish plaster specifically designed for creating a skim coat on plasterboard.

Do-it-yourself plasters

The one thing that all "professional" plasters have in common is that they are difficult to apply. They come in large unwieldy bags and have to be mixed with water; they normally set more quickly than the do-it-yourself enthusiast can cope with; it is easy to drag them off the wall when you are applying them; you need a lot of practice to obtain a smooth, even finish; and generally they can be put on only in thin layers.

Do-it-yourself plasters have been specifically designed to overcome all these problems. Two grades are available, repair and finish, and are usually available ready-mixed in small tubs, although sometimes as a powder for mixing with water.

Repair or one-coat plaster is much easier to apply than conventional undercoat plaster and can be used in thicknesses up to 50mm (2in). It can be employed either for filling deep holes – the kind you might be left with when a waste pipe has been removed from a wall – or to provide a base for the

ABOVE Some do-it-yourself finish plasters can be applied with a paintbrush.

Applying plaster

1 Mix do-it-yourself repair plaster in a bucket. Always add powder to water.

2 Scoop do-it-yourself repair plaster from the hawk with a plasterer's trowel.

3 Apply do-it-yourself repair plaster to a wall using a plasterer's trowel.

4 Level out the plaster with a straight length of wood, worked from side to side.

finish plaster, although do-it-yourself repair plasters are often smooth enough on their own as a basis for wall tiles and many wallpapers.

Do-it-yourself finish plaster, also known as plaster skim, can be applied up to 3mm (⅛ in) thick. As well as providing a finish over repair plaster, it can also be used for smoothing a rough surface and for covering over plasterboard.

How to apply plaster

All types of plaster can be applied with a plasterer's trowel. Carry the plaster to the wall on a hawk, a square flat board mounted on a short handle, and lift a small quantity of plaster off the hawk on to the wall using the plasterer's trowel. Spread it

out with a sweeping motion. Always keep the trowel blade at an angle to the wall and allow the plaster to squeeze out through the gap between the bottom blade edge and the wall. When the plaster is starting to dry, it can be smoothed over, holding the trowel at an angle.

To ensure that a plaster repair is flush with the surrounding plaster, use a straight-edged length of wood and smooth over with a side-to-side motion, resting the ends on the nearby dry plaster surface.

Finish plaster is applied in the same way, but is polished with a flat trowel when almost dry. Some finishing plasters are applied with a brush, although a plastic spreader will be needed to give it a final smoothing.

External corners

If you need to apply plaster to an external corner, secure metal beading to the corner first, using dabs of plaster.

ABOVE On external corners, plaster should be applied over a corner bead.

Plasterboard

In a timber-framed house, the inner surfaces of exterior walls will be plasterboard (gypsum board), which is solid plaster contained by paper, as will the surfaces of all internal dividing walls. These may be given a skim coat of plaster to cover up the joints between adjacent sheets of plasterboard, or they can have the joints and nail holes filled before painting or papering. Some interior dividing walls in masonry walled houses may comprise plasterboard mounted on timber frames.

Replastering a bricked-up doorway

1 Remove any loose or crumbling plaster from the sides and top of the doorway.

2 Apply the first layer of undercoat plaster over wire mesh no more than 10mm (⅜in) thick.

3 Make scratches in the first layer to provide a "key" for the second layer of undercoat.

4 Apply the second layer of undercoat plaster and level it off with a timber straightedge.

5 When dry, apply the final layer of finishing plaster. Polish it smooth with a flat trowel.

CONCRETE AND MORTAR

Concrete is used to provide a solid and rigid surface as a floor, as paving or as a base for a garage or outbuilding. Mortar is the "glue" that holds the bricks together in a wall. The basis for both concrete and mortar is cement and sand (fine aggregate); concrete also contains stones (coarse aggregate). When mixed with water, the cement sets to bind the aggregates together.

CEMENT

Most cement used in the home is OPC (Ordinary Portland Cement). This is air-setting (that is, moisture in the air will cause it to harden unless bags are kept sealed). Ordinary Portland Cement is grey in colour and is sold in standard 50kg (112lb or 1cwt) bags in the UK, although smaller sizes are often available. Occasionally, two other types of cement are used in and around the home, White Portland Cement and Masonry Cement. The former is used where appearance is important, while the latter contains additives to increase the workability of mortars and renders.

AGGREGATES

Coarse aggregates are defined as those that will pass through a 20mm (¾in) sieve and are widely used for making concrete. Fine aggregates are often known simply as sand and are used in both concrete and mortar.

Two different types of sand are sold for building work. Sharp sand, sometimes known as concreting sand, is used for making concrete and mortar for laying paving slabs; soft sand, also known as bricklaying or building sand, is used in mortar for laying bricks and concrete blocks. You can also obtain all-in aggregate, often known as ballast, which contains both coarse and fine aggregates.

BUYING CONCRETE AND MORTAR

There are three ways of buying concrete and mortar: as individual ingredients, as wet ready-mixed and as dry pre-mixed. Buying cement, sand and coarse aggregate separately for concrete is the cheapest option, but you do have to ensure dry storage for the cement. For big jobs, having wet ready-mixed concrete delivered is convenient, provided sufficient manpower is available to transport it from the truck to the site and to level it before it sets. For small jobs, bags of dry pre-mix are a good choice: the ingredients are in the correct proportions, and all you do is add water.

MIXING CONCRETE

1 Start by measuring out the dry ingredients in the right proportions.

2 Mix the dry ingredients thoroughly until you have a consistent colour.

3 Make a small well in the centre of the pile and add a small amount of water.

4 Work from the edges of the pile, mixing the ingredients and adding more water.

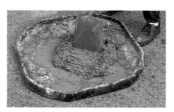

5 Work the material with the edge of your spade to get the right consistency.

6 When the concrete is mixed, transfer it to a bucket or wheelbarrow.

ADDITIVES

Pigments can be added to the mix to change the colour of concrete, but need using with care. The most common additives affect the workability of concrete and mortar and often increase the time before it hardens. Many mortars need the addition of lime or a plasticizer to improve their workability.

CONCRETE AND MORTAR MIXES

The proportions of cement, sand and aggregate you need depend on the job you are doing: strong mixes are those with more cement; weak mixes are those with less. All proportions are by volume.

General-purpose concrete Good for most uses, except foundations and exposed paving. Mix one part cement, two parts sand and three parts 20mm (¾in) aggregate, or one part cement to four parts combined aggregate. This mix is known as 1:2:3 or 1:4.

Foundation concrete Use for wall foundations and bases and for precast paving. Mix 1:2½:3½ or 1:5.

Paving concrete Use for all exposed paving, especially drives, and garage floors. Mix 1:1½:2½ or 1:3½.

Normal mortar Use for bricklaying in normal conditions. Mix 1:5 to 6 (cement: soft sand) with a small amount of plasticizer or one part lime added for workability, or 1:4 to 5 (masonry cement: soft sand).

Strong mortar Use for brick walls in exposed conditions. Mix 1:4 to 4½ (cement: sand) with plasticizer or a quarter part lime added, or 1:2½ to 3½ (masonry cement: sand).

MIXING CONCRETE AND MORTAR

Even with bags of dry pre-mix, you will need a spot board, usually a sheet of hardboard or plywood, to mix the material with water.

Start by mixing the ingredients thoroughly. Measure out separate cement, sand and aggregate using a bucket in their dry state. Make a well in the centre of the pile and add some water using a different bucket.

Work material from the edges of the pile into the wet centre. Then make another well and add a little more water. Continue mixing and adding small quantities of water until it is all mixed and a uniform colour. The consistency is correct when you can just draw the back of your spade across it, leaving a smooth finish without water oozing out.

For large jobs, consider hiring a mixer. For concrete, start with half of the aggregate and water, then add the cement and sand in small batches plus the remainder of the aggregate and water. Clean the mixer with a small amount of coarse aggregate and clean water. A powered mortar mixer can also be hired to speed up the mixing process.

CONCRETE AND MORTAR MIXES						
CONCRETE	**MIX**	**CEMENT**	**SAND**	**AGGREGATE**	**YIELD***	**AREA****
General-purpose	1:2:3	50kg (110lb)	100kg (220lb)	200kg (440lb)	0.15 (5.3)	1.5 (16)
Foundation	1:2½:3½	50kg (110lb)	130kg (290lb)	200kg (440lb)	0.18 (6.4)	1.8 (19.4)
Paving	1:1½:2½	50kg (110lb)	75kg (165lb)	150kg (330lb)	0.12 (4.2)	1.2 (13)
MORTAR				**LIME****		**BRICKS LAID**
Normal	1:5	50kg (110lb)	200kg (440lb)	50kg (110lb)	0.25 (8.8)	850
Strong	1:4	50kg (110lb)	150kg (330lb)	15kg (33lb)	0.19 (6.7)	650

* cubic metres (cubic feet) per 50kg (110lb) of cement

** area in square metres (square feet) of concrete 100mm (4in) thick

*** or plasticizer

ABOVE A powered concrete mixer can also be hired to speed up the mixing process. Empty the concrete into a wheelbarrow.

ROOFING MATERIALS

Two shapes of roof are used on houses: pitched and flat. Each employs different covering materials, although the basic framework is timber in both cases. If you are thinking about changing the roof covering on your house, bear in mind the style of other houses in the area and the weight of the roofing material the roof was designed for.

PITCHED ROOFS

A pitched roof has a series of rafters supported at the bottom by the house walls and joined to a horizontal board at the ridge. Thin timber battens (furring strips) are nailed across the rafters to support the roof covering. Normally, felt is laid beneath the battens for additional weatherproofing, and some roofs have boards, known as sarking, below the felt. The main cladding materials are natural slate, manufactured slate and concrete and clay tiles.

Some roofs may have more than one pitch – on L-shaped houses and houses with front gables for example. Each section of the roof is covered separately; a lead-lined valley runs between the sections to collect rainwater.

FLAT ROOFS

These actually have a gentle slope to remove rainwater. They are constructed from timber boards laid on top of joists, the boards being covered with asphalt or roofing felt. Felt is also used on the pitched roofs of outbuildings and sheds.

NATURAL SLATES

Although widely used on older houses, natural slates have become very expensive and are now rarely used as a new roofing material. However, second-hand slates can often be obtained for small jobs, repairs and replacement.

LEFT A professional roofer at work constructing this well-insulated roof. The horizontal battens have yet to be fitted; the vertical battens will provide ventilation to keep the sarking underneath dry.

Slates are held to the roofing battens by nails – either through two holes near the top of the slate (head nailing) or two holes in the middle of the slate (centre nailing). In both cases, each slate covers about two-thirds of the two slates below it, so that all of the roof is covered by a thickness of at least two slates.

Natural slates are heavy and require handling with great care – they are fragile and have sharp edges.

ABOVE Architectural salvage yards are the best place to find old slates and tiles.

The nail holes can be made with an electric drill fitted with a masonry drill bit, though a professional slater uses the spike on his axe.

Natural stone roofing, which is even more expensive, is laid in the same way as slates.

PLAIN TILES

Clay plain tiles are another traditional material, but they are laid in a different manner – each tile has two

ABOVE This "eyebrow" roof is made from plain concrete tiles.

FAR LEFT Modern
concrete inter-
locking tiles on both
house and garage.
This style is known
as "Double Roman".

LEFT Manufactured
slates do not just
have to be used on
old roofs. Here, they
are ideal for this
modern building.

projecting lugs, known as nibs, on
the back, which hook over the
roofing battens. Some tiles are nailed
in place as well, typically every
fourth row and the tiles at the top,
bottom and edges of the roof.

As with slates, each tile covers
around two-thirds the length of the
tiles underneath – thus the amount
exposed is about one-third of the
total tile length.

Plain clay tiles need a more steeply
pitched roof than slates – a
minimum of 40 degrees compared
to around 20 degrees.

Plain concrete tiles are also
available and are held on the battens
in the same way as clay tiles.

INTERLOCKING TILES

Concrete tiles that are interlocking
are widely used on modern homes
and have yet another method of
fixing. Like plain tiles, they hook
over the roofing battens, but also
interlock, each with its two
neighbours, so that only one layer is
needed and each tile only covers a
small part of the tiles below.

There are many types of interlocking tile and the minimum pitch
can vary from under 20 degrees to
around 30 degrees. Interlocking clay
tiles are also available, including
decorative pantiles. To make replacement easy, the name and number
may be embossed on the back.

MANUFACTURED SLATES

Lighter, cheaper and easier to lay,
manufactured slates have largely
replaced natural slates. Made from
resin, they often contain ground
natural slate and may have "deckled"
edges for a more realistic
appearance. Many are held in place
with clips, which makes them much
easier to lay, although the roof itself
needs to be truer in construction
than is needed for natural slates.

SHINGLES

These are wooden tiles used for
cladding walls and also for covering
roofs. They are usually made from
Western Red Cedar, which weathers
naturally to a silver-grey colour.
They are particularly suitable for use
on steeply pitched roofs and are
fixed in the same way as slates.

FLAT ROOFING MATERIALS

Roofing felt varies in quality from
simple bitumen sheet felt, employed
for outbuildings, to expensive and
long-lasting polyester felt used for
garage roofs. New felt roofs for
houses are often laid with hot
bitumen – a job for professionals, as
is laying a hot asphalt roof covering.

RIGHT It would be
difficult to find a
more elegant roof
covering than
natural slate for this
traditional-style
building. To add
contrasting colour,
the ridge tiles are
made from clay.

GUTTERING

These perform the very useful function of collecting the rainwater that falls on roofs and transferring it to underground drains. The size, shape and materials used can vary. The traditional material used for guttering was cast iron, but this has largely been replaced by plastic. Other materials that may be found include aluminium, galvanized steel and asbestos cement.

GUTTERING COMPONENTS

These can have one of three main shapes: half-round, square or moulded – ogee moulded is the traditional shape. Whatever its shape, most guttering comes in standard lengths, so it needs joints between the lengths. Each length will be supported by two or more brackets; some brackets are combined with joint units.

At a corner, a right-angle (90-degree) elbow joins two lengths together – 120- and 135-degree elbows are also available for bay windows – and at the edge of the roof, a stop-end is fitted. The gutter is connected via an outlet to the downpipe, which takes the rainwater to the drains; if this is at the end of the gutter, it is known as a stop-end outlet. The downpipe has its own brackets and elbows, plus some kind of outlet at the bottom to direct the water into the drainage gulley. Sometimes, and especially where there is more than one downpipe, a hopper head is fitted to a single downpipe and pipes from the gutters empty their water into the hopper head to be taken to the drains.

For the majority of houses, 115mm (4½in) guttering is used in combination with 70mm (2¾in) downpipes. On large houses, deep-flow guttering, with a greater capacity, is used. On garages, extensions and outbuildings, 75mm (3in) guttering plus 50mm (2in) downpipes will suffice.

LEFT Whatever type of guttering you choose for your home, keep to the same make and type for the whole house.

CAST-IRON GUTTERING

Although cast-iron is a rigid and a durable material, it is very heavy and brittle, and liable to rust if not kept painted. It is available in half-round and ogee profiles with a choice of round and square downpipes. Ornate cast-iron hopper heads are available, both new and second-hand.

The joints between lengths of gutter are made by the spigot of one length fitting into the socket of the next, with a layer of putty providing a waterproof seal between them once a bolt and nut have been used to lock the two lengths together.

ALUMINIUM GUTTERING

As a guttering material, aluminium has the advantage of being rigid and rustproof. Normally, it comes pre-finished in a range of colours and in a wide choice of profiles.

BELOW Here, the rainwater that falls from the top roof descends on to the lower roof where it is collected by the lower gutter. It then descends the lower downpipe to the drains.

PLASTIC GUTTERING

Although less rigid than cast-iron and aluminium guttering, plastic guttering does not corrode, and is light and easy to handle.

Plastic guttering is available in a choice of colours. Half-round and square are the most common profiles, and are available in standard and deep-flow patterns, although both moulded and ogee forms are also available. Connectors are available for joining to existing plastic or cast-iron guttering; downpipes can be round, square or rectangular. Some half-round guttering is ribbed so that leaves can fall into the gutter, but water can still flow underneath them.

Plastic guttering may be sealed by rubber or neoprene gaskets fitted into the connectors; the gutters themselves are a simple snap-fit into the brackets, although sometimes notches need to be cut in the gutter to fit connectors.

Although they may have the same nominal size and the same profile, different makes of plastic guttering are often not compatible with one another. It is advisable to stick with one make and use it for all the guttering around your house.

FITTING GUTTERING

Many guttering manufacturers provide excellent literature, which will help you select replacement guttering for your home and give full instructions on how it should be fitted. One of the most important aspects is that the guttering has the capacity to cope with the amount of rainwater that falls on the house. It also needs to be laid with a slight fall from the highest point, usually the

RIGHT Just some of the different shapes and sizes of plastic guttering available from a single manufacturer.

BELOW RIGHT If you are fitting guttering yourself, always have a good work platform beneath you and wear the correct safety equipment.

roof edge, to the lowest point, always the outlet to the downpipe. Check with your local authority or council for what arrangements are acceptable when getting rid of the rainwater.

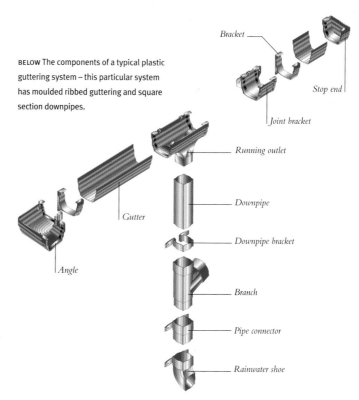

BELOW The components of a typical plastic guttering system – this particular system has moulded ribbed guttering and square section downpipes.

Bracket

Stop end

Joint bracket

Running outlet

Downpipe

Downpipe bracket

Branch

Pipe connector

Rainwater shoe

Gutter

Angle

Adhesives and Sealants

A fantastic range of adhesives and sealants is available, some designed for specific uses, woodworking adhesive and bath sealant for example, and others formulated for more general use. You need a good selection of both adhesives and sealants in your do-it-yourself armoury, some of which you buy when you need them, others you keep in reserve for emergencies.

Woodworking adhesives

The majority of woodwork projects that require two or more pieces of wood to be glued together need a PVA (white) woodworking adhesive. This white liquid dries quickly, loses its colour, and has the advantage that excess adhesive can be removed with a damp cloth before it sets.

Where a joint has to withstand damp conditions, an exterior-grade of woodworking adhesive must be used; if the joint may need to be taken apart in the future, a traditional woodworking adhesive, such as animal glue or fish glue, can be used.

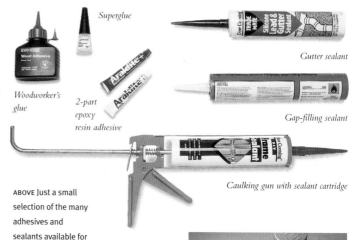

Superglue

Woodworker's glue

2-part epoxy resin adhesive

Gutter sealant

Gap-filling sealant

Caulking gun with sealant cartridge

ABOVE Just a small selection of the many adhesives and sealants available for various types of job.

Two-part adhesives

These adhesives can be used on a wide range of materials and are very useful, as they are strong and can fill gaps between the two mating surfaces, which is often necessary when repairing broken china. Some two-part adhesives are even suitable for joining metal. For epoxy resin types, the two parts come in separate tubes and must be mixed together just before use; for two-part acrylic types, the adhesive is applied to one surface and the hardener to the other. Quick-setting versions are available, although drying time does depend on temperature, the warmer the better. You may need to experiment with different types when trying to glue plastics together.

ABOVE A range of household glues and tape for repair work.

ABOVE A PVA woodworking adhesive used to join two boards together.

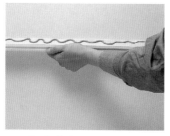

ABOVE Panel adhesive can be used to secure timber mouldings to walls.

ABOVE A two-part epoxy adhesive is ideal for repairing broken china.

Contact adhesives

This type of adhesive is used for joining sheet materials, for example, plastic laminate sheet to a timber worktop, and for repairing leather. Adhesive is applied to both surfaces and allowed to dry until it becomes tacky, then the surfaces are brought together. Some contact adhesives allow slight adjustment after the surfaces have been joined; with others, you have to get the positioning right the first time. Take care when using solvent-based contact adhesives, do not smoke and ensure there is adequate ventilation.

Superglue

This type of adhesive has the advantage that it sets almost immediately, so you can actually hold the two parts to be glued rather than fitting clamps, straps or weights. It has no gap-filling properties and no flexibility when set, but nevertheless is extremely useful. Make sure you have the correct release agent to hand in case you get any on your skin as it can glue fingers together.

Special adhesives

Some adhesives should only be bought when needed. These include:
• Glass adhesive that sets clear under the action of light with no obvious glue line.
• Panel adhesive, for securing manufactured boards.
• Specialized adhesives for wallpapering and tiling.
• Adhesives for repairing PVC.
• Specialized adhesives for laying soft floorcoverings.

Sealants

The majority of sealants come in cartridges designed to fit into a caulking gun. This is an essential, but inexpensive, tool and is easy to use after a little practice. If you retain the tip that you cut off the end of the cartridge nozzle before you can use it, it can be reversed and used to seal the cartridge after use.

The most useful sealants for use around the home are the building silicones and mastics (caulking), available in different colours and different grades depending on the final use. These have the advantage that they never set completely, so can be used for sealing between two materials that are likely to move slightly. Common examples are the gap between a bath, basin or shower tray and a wall, and the gap between a window or door frame and the surrounding brickwork; a rigid sealant or filler used here would crack quite quickly.

Various repair sealants, often incorporating bitumen, are available for mending cracks in gutters, downpipes and flat roofs; expanding foam fillers can be used for sealing really large gaps.

Practical tip

• When using most types of adhesive (superglues are the exception), you will need to clamp at least two surfaces together while the adhesive dries. Work out your clamping arrangement before applying the adhesive, so that you are certain that the two (or more) parts will be held together securely.

ABOVE Use mastic or silicon sealant indoors and outdoors to seal gaps between wood and masonry where a rigid filler might crack.

ABOVE Use a non-setting mastic or coloured building silicone sealant to fill gaps around a door frame.

ABOVE Use white waterproof sealant for the gap behind a wash basin. Apply it in one continuous movement.

Timber and Manufactured Boards

Do-it-yourself projects rarely involve expensive hardwoods such as mahogany, oak, ash and beech. These tend to be used by furniture makers and the joinery trade, owing to their high cost and relative difficulty in working. Softwoods, such as prepared pine, or manufactured boards are the basic materials used by the home craftsperson for most structural work.

Using wood

Hardwoods, as they are expensive, are often used as veneers over cheaper materials, as lippings around flat surfaces such as shelving and table tops, and for picture framing.

Softwoods, such as pine and, to a lesser extent, Douglas fir, are the most commonly used types of wood for do-it-yourself jobs such as wall frames, flooring, skirting (base) boards, picture and dado (chair) rails and a great variety of cladding, framing and fencing applications.

In addition to softwoods, there is a range of manufactured boards, which are cheap and come in convenient sizes that keep jointing to the minimum.

Practical uses

The two manufactured boards most often used are plywood and chipboard (particle board). The former, which has good mechanical strength and can be sawn easily, is suitable for structural work.

ABOVE A selection of manufactured boards.

Chipboard is more friable and less easy to work accurately, but is cheap. It is adequate for some flooring applications and a host of carcassing jobs, such as kitchen cabinets and bookcases. It is unwise to drive screws or nails into the edge of a chipboard panel, as the material will crumble.

Veneered finishes

Both plywood and chipboard are available with hardwood and coloured melamine veneer for improved appearance.

Practical tip

- Like many manufactured boards, hardboard does not like damp conditions and has a tendency to buckle. Keep it away from steamy areas if possible, or make sure it is sealed with paint, polyurethane varnish or proprietary sealer.

Blockboard, which consists of solid wooden blocks sandwiched between plywood skins, is a stable and strong structural material often used where some form of weight-carrying capacity is required. As with all manufactured boards, the extremely hard resins used to bond blockboard together rapidly blunts tools unless they are tungsten (carbide) tipped.

Pineboard is like the core of blockboard, but without the outer layers. Small strips of pine are glued together on edge and sanded smooth. It is ideal for instant shelving and carcassing.

MDF (medium-density fibreboard) is another useful material. Unlike

Common thickness of manufactured board

Type	3mm ⅛in	6mm ¼in	9mm ⅜in	12mm ½in	16mm ⅝in	19mm ¾in	22mm ⅞in	25mm 1in	32mm 1¼in
Plywood	x	x	x	x	x	x	x	x	
Plywood (D. Fir)				x		x			
Blockboard						x		x	
Chipboard				x	x	x	x	x	
Hardboard	x	x							
MDF		x	x	x		x		x	x

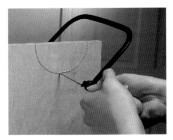

ABOVE Plywood is easy to cut and is very good for carcassing work.

ABOVE Sawing veneered chipboard is best done with the veneer face-up to avoid damage.

ABOVE Cutting a template from hardboard using an electric jigsaw.

most other boards, it can be worked to fine detail with saws and chisels, and it is often used for making quite delicate mouldings. Hardboard is ideal for covering floors prior to tiling or carpeting and, as it is light, for making back panels for cabinets or pictures. It can be used for making templates to establish correct shapes,

especially when using expensive material for the finished object, helping to avoid mistakes.

DIFFERENT USES FOR WOOD

Hardwoods, such as mahogany, oak, ash and beech, are readily available, but tend to be used in the furniture trades for making solid items such as chairs, which have few flat surfaces and need structural strength. Boards with hardwood veneers are often used for panelling and other flat surfaces such as table tops and interior doors.

Typical applications for softwoods include flooring, internal doors, skirtings and framing for projects that will be clad with a variety of materials. Tongued-and-grooved cladding has become popular over the years. It provides a relatively inexpensive decorative finish using solid timber. Tongued-and-grooved timber comes in a variety of species but the most commonly found is pine or a similar softwood such as hemlock. More exotic species will need to be specially ordered.

ABOVE LEFT The centre section of this display case was made from MDF and then painted.

LEFT The carcass of this bookcase is a box made of veneered MDF with solid wood trim.

BELOW A skirting (base) board, veneers, softwoods and hardwoods.

Paper-coated MDF skirting (base) board

Bird's-eye maple veneer   *Cherry veneer*

Pine softwood   *Douglas fir softwood*

Beech hardwood   *Mahogany hardwood*

Floor Coverings

Whether you have a solid concrete floor or a suspended timber floor, there is a wide range of floor coverings to choose from. Floor coverings can be divided into five main groups, including carpet; sheet materials, mainly vinyl and linoleum; soft floor tiles including vinyl, cork, rubber, linoleum and carpet tiles; hard floor tiles such as ceramic and quarry tiles; and timber floors.

Carpet

There are two main types of carpet: fabric-backed and foam-backed. The former requires special edge gripper strips and an underlay, and is difficult for an amateur to lay successfully, as it has to be stretched as it is laid. The latter requires no underlay, except paper to cover gaps in floorboards, and is easy to cut and to lay, using double-sided adhesive tape.

Carpet comes in a vast range of designs and qualities, and in different grades for a variety of situations: the heaviest wear grades are required in hallways and on stairs; the lowest grades in bedrooms. Water-resistant grades are needed in bathrooms. Carpet, except carpet tiles, is not recommended for kitchens.

Sheet materials

Vinyl sheet flooring is easy to cut, easy to lay and easy to keep clean, making it ideal for use in bathrooms, kitchens and children's bedrooms.

LEFT A linoleum floor is ideal for kitchens as it is very durable and easy to keep clean. The cushioned types also offer extra warmth and softness underfoot. Borders can be used to frame individual tiles.

Normal sheet vinyl is reasonably soft and warm underfoot, cushion vinyl even more so.

Durable linoleum (oil-impregnated sheet) is the traditional sheet flooring, but is more difficult to lay. However, modern linos come in a range of patterns and colourful designs that rival vinyl sheeting.

Soft floor tiles

All soft floor tiles are quiet, warm and comfortable underfoot. As they are also easy to clean, they are suitable for bathrooms, kitchens work rooms and bedrooms.

All soft floor tile materials must be laid on a surface that is absolutely dry and flat: a solid concrete floor

ABOVE A variety of natural floor coverings such as sea grass.

ABOVE Carpet tiles can be laid with any pattern.

ABOVE A selection of soft floor coverings, including cork.

ABOVE There is a vast array of hard flooring tiles available.

will probably require levelling, while a timber floor may need covering with sheets of hardboard.

Most soft floor tiles are laid in the same way. Individual tiles are stuck to the floor using the correct adhesive or by peeling off the backing from self-adhesive tiles. In general, carpet tiles are laid dry, with perhaps just a few secured with double-sided adhesive tape to keep the whole floor in place.

HARD FLOOR TILES

These materials are also easy to keep clean, so they can be used in the same rooms as soft floor tiles. They are much more durable, but are cold underfoot and noisy.

The main materials are ceramic (glazed clay), and quarry or terracotta. Ceramic floor tiles, which are thicker and stronger than ceramic wall tiles, are laid with a special adhesive, and grout is used to fill the gaps between them. Quarry and terracotta tiles are laid with a cement mortar, which is also used to fill the gaps. Hard floor tiles need a rigid, dry, flat surface. On a timber floor, this means laying thin plywood sheeting rather than hardboard.

LEFT Quarry tiles are unglazed ceramic floor tiles with a brown, buff or reddish colour, and are a very popular choice for hallways, conservatories and country-style kitchens. Terracotta tiles are featured here.

TIMBER FLOOR COVERINGS

There are many timber floor coverings that can be laid on top of existing floors. Some are nailed down, some are stuck down and some are allowed to "float", not actually being secured to the floor underneath, but being free to expand and contract independently.

Timber flooring is available in thin strips, sometimes two or three boards wide, resembling floorboards. The strips are tongued and grooved and are glued together, but not to the floor underneath. Thicker timber strips can be laid in the same way, but can also be nailed to the floor below. Although some thick strips are made of hardwood, this timber is so expensive that in some cases, laminate flooring (a thin hardwood layer attached to a thick softwood layer) is used. Timber mosaic flooring, often known as imitation parquet flooring, consists of square tiles that

are glued to the underlying floor; most types are self-adhesive. Each tile consists of four smaller tiles, and each smaller tile comprises a number of small timber "fingers", so the final effect is a basketweave design. True parquet flooring consists of thick blocks that are glued to the floor, typically using a black mastic (caulking), in a herringbone pattern. Achieving a flat level surface with this type of flooring is not easy. Timber floorboards themselves can be made to look good if varnished.

LEFT Woodstrip, laminated and mosaic flooring.

RIGHT A wooden floor can be warm and stylish.

Fixings

Often, home improvement projects involve joining together materials with very different properties, such as fixing wood to brickwork or plaster, or metal to brickwork or stone. The problems arising from this can be overcome in a variety of ways, not least by taking advantage of the many different fixings manufactured for use with new materials and hollow walls.

Choosing fixings

Different types of fixing are required for hollow walls. Fixing wood to wood can be done in a variety of ways, including nailing, screwing and gluing, but there are many proprietary brackets, plates and knock-down joints that can make the job much quicker and often stronger. Knock-down joints also allow a project to be dismantled and reassembled at will. Often do-it-yourself projects can be made or marred by the choice of fixings, especially where they are visible. A good general rule is to make them as simple as possible, both visually and mechanically, particularly when choosing catches for cabinets and door furniture in general.

As a rule of thumb, never use a fixing that is too large or ostentatious so as to detract from the item of furniture.

RIGHT Fixing a batten (furring strip) to an exterior wall with a masonry nail is now a commonly applied method.

BELOW A cordless drill and a selection of wall plugs and screws.

Cordless drill/driver

Wall plugs and screws: sizes 6/8/10 to fit a 6mm (¼in) drill diameter

Wall plugs and screws: sizes 4/6/8/10 to fit a 5mm (³⁄₁₆in) drill diameter

Wall plugs and screws: sizes 10/12/14 to fit a 7mm (¼in) drill diameter

Masonry nails

These provide the most basic method of attaching timber to brickwork and plaster. They are hardened nails that can be driven into masonry and give a firm fixing. They are not used in the assembly of a wooden structure, but simply hold it to the wall.

Fixings for solid walls

Plastic wall plugs are the most common method of providing fixings in solid walls. They expand to grip the sides of the hole when a wood screw is driven home. They must be a snug fit in their holes, otherwise they will not hold. Wall plugs come in various sizes and are designed for moderate loads, such as shelves, curtain rails, mirrors etc.

Frame fixers are made specifically for fixing door and window frames directly to the masonry in one operation. They comprise a long wall plug, often supplied with a

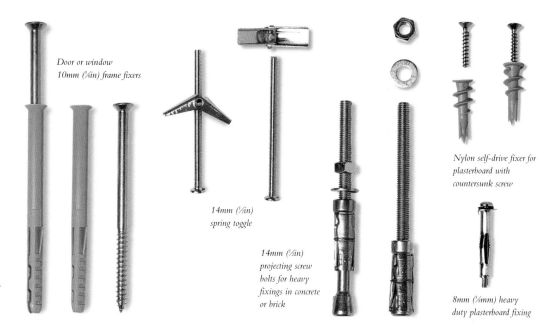

Door or window
10mm (⅜in) frame fixers

14mm (½in)
spring toggle

14mm (½in)
projecting screw
bolts for heavy
fixings in concrete
or brick

Nylon self-drive fixer for
plasterboard with
countersunk screw

8mm (⅜mm) heavy
duty plasterboard fixing

screw of the correct size. A hole is drilled through the frame with a wood drill and continued into the brickwork with a masonry drill. The fixer is tapped through the frame into the wall and the screw tightened in the normal way. Some types can be hammered home, but they will still need to be undone with a screwdriver.

Screw bolts are often used where a heavy load is expected, such as when fitting heavy timbers to brickwork. The bolt expands within the hole as the nut is tightened, providing a very strong grip. A washer should always be used under the nut to prevent damage to the wood as it is tightened since these exert a very strong grip.

Fixings for hollow walls and doors
Cavity fixings are designed to expand to grip the inner surface of

chipboard (particle board) or hollow doors and are sufficient to hold moderate loads. They can also be used with lath-and-plaster walls often found in older buildings.

Spring toggles work in a similar way to other cavity fixings. They are pushed into the hole with the springs in compression and once the arms have passed through, they spring open to grip the back of the surface material. The device is then tightened with a screwdriver.

Often used for light fixings in plasterboard (gypsum board), the self-drive fixer taps its own thread in a hole drilled slightly smaller than the diameter of the plug. The plug will remain in place even when the fixing screw is removed.

Plasterboard can present its own particular problems with fixings owing to its fragile and crumbly nature. The golden rule is to get it right the first time.

ABOVE A range of fixings designed to overcome problems of getting a secure fixing in very different materials. Most of these have appeared in the last 40 years or so, and manufacturers continue to develop and improve quality constantly.

PRACTICAL TIPS

• Always wear safety goggles when using masonry nails because, if struck incorrectly, they will not bend like a wire nail and may shatter and cause injury.

• Make sure that all fixings made in plaster are made when the material is dry, otherwise shrinkage may well cause problems later.

• Shelving designed to carry heavy weights will be heavy itself, and its weight should be considered when deciding on the fixings required.

Joints and Hinges

There is a huge range of fittings available for making joints and connecting different materials. Any device that includes a pivot action can be called a hinge, and there are many different variations. Some are designed to be concealed within the framework of a cabinet, or the carcass, while others are intended as decorative features in their own right.

JOINT PLATES AND BRACKETS

Flat mild-steel plates, drilled and countersunk to take wood screws, are a common means of making and strengthening butt joints in timber framing. Fixings are also available to make right-angled joints, lap joints, and for hanging joists.

Another very handy fixing is the trestle dog. With a pair of these and some timber, you can make a trestle. They are also useful for assembling impromptu benches and small scaffolds in a few minutes. The greater the weight they bear, the harder they grip.

SHELVING AIDS

Simple metal brackets are readily available. They are fixed to the wall with screws and wall plugs, and then a wooden shelf is secured from

below with screws. Shaped wooden brackets give a traditional look and are plugged to the wall in a similar way. Glass shelving for the bathroom may be fixed with shelf-grips, which are backed with adhesive strips for securing to ceramic tiles. Shelves over radiators are often of coated steel with a wood-grain decorative finish. They simply clip into place over the radiators.

Heavy-duty wall brackets are required to hold the weight of a television. These are made of metal and allow the television to be rotated through 360 degrees and tilted downward. Shelving systems are available from many sources. Often, they offer great flexibility and lots of add-on accessories. Many can be used as room dividers and as portable furniture.

ABOVE Trestle dogs provide a quick way of joining wood for an immediate work platform.

OPPOSITE A selection of the many different types and sizes of hinges that can be found, available in a variety of finishes.

BELOW Various traditional ways of joining timbers with metal brackets.

L-shaped corner reinforcing bracket

T-shaped fixing plate

L-shaped bracket

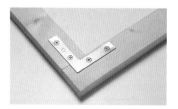

A simple 90 degree angle bracket

An ideal method used in crossing joints

A butt joint held on either side with brackets

KNOCK-DOWN JOINTS

These joints are often used with manufactured boards, such as chipboard (particle board) and plywood. They ensure good square connections and allow the unit to be dismantled and reassembled as required. For the best results, at least two should be used for every panel.

HINGES

There is a wide range of hinges in a choice of types, finishes, sizes and materials for a variety of tasks; some are functional, while others make decorative features in their own right. Many specialist outlets sell all manner of hinges, stays and catches, and most can be ordered by mail.

The selection of the correct hinges for a job is important, since they must be able to support the

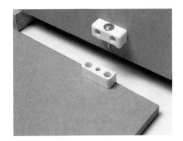

ABOVE The knock-down joint in its separate parts ready for putting together.

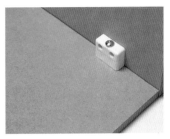

ABOVE When the parts are joined, they form a strong and accurate joint.

weight of the door, which could be quite considerable if it is an external door. Butt hinges are the most common type.

Special chipboard concealed hinges are a familiar sight on furniture such as kitchen cabinets. In the case of a bar counter, they must be able to fold back flat. For internal doors, rising-butt hinges will allow the

door to rise as it is opened so that it clears a thick carpet, yet lets in no draught when closed.

CATCHES

These are usually made very simply and are more often seen on cabinets and garden gates than on fancy furniture. Modern ones are often sprung ball bearings.

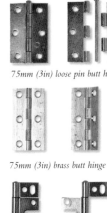

75mm (3in) loose pin butt hinge

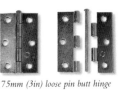

75mm (3in) brass butt hinge

75mm (3in) fasfit hinge

25mm (1in) steel backflap hinge

75mm (3in) rising butt hinge

100mm (4in) stainless steel butt hinge

100mm (4in) brass security butt hinge

Screw-in barrel hinge with finials

75mm (3in) tee hinge

Easy hang, zinc-plated hinge

58mm (2¼in) brass butterfly hinge

75 x 14mm (3 x ⁹⁄₁₆in) steel strap hinge

50mm (2in) antiqued brass H-hinge

26mm (1in) concealed, steel unsprung hinge

Brass turn button

Cupboard catch

12mm (½in) bales (ball) catch

Painting Equipment

This is one aspect of do-it-yourself work where you cannot afford to skimp on materials. You will not achieve professional results by using cheap brushes that shed their bristles as you work, or cut-price rollers that disintegrate before the job is finished. Invest in the best quality equipment your budget allows if you are serious about your work.

Choosing brushes

Paintbrushes come in pure bristle, synthetic fibre and even foam versions. The last guarantees that you will not be left with brush strokes, and they are inexpensive enough to discard when you have finished. All natural brushes shed a few bristles in use, but cheap brushes are the worst offenders. Usually, these have fewer bristles to start with and they are often poorly secured. Regard pure bristle brushes as an investment; you can reuse them repeatedly, and many professional painters claim that their performance improves with age.

Synthetic brushes, usually with nylon bristles, have the big advantage of being moult-free, and they perform well with water-based paints. A more expensive version, made of polyester and nylon, is particularly easy to handle and said to give a superior finish.

Tool box essentials

Serious painters will need a range of brushes: slimline, 12 and 25mm (½ and 1in), for fiddly areas, such as window frames; medium sized versions, 50 and 75mm (2 and 3in), for doors, floors and skirting (base) boards; and large types, 100mm (4in), for quick coverage of walls and ceilings. You might like to add a few extras to this basic kit:

• A cutting-in (sash) brush, specially angled to cope with hard-to-reach areas, is particularly useful if you are painting around window frames. It comes in 12mm, 18mm and 25mm (½, ¾ and 1in) versions.

Practical tips

• Work new brushes across your palm to dislodge any loose bristles.

• Use an extension pole with your roller when painting ceilings.

• Imagine you are holding a pen when using lightweight brushes; this gives maximum control.

• A radiator brush, available with a plastic or metal handle and designed to reach the wall behind a radiator.
• Special-effects brushes, from stubby stencil brushes to mottlers, which allow you to create the distinctive look of woodgrain, and a range of artist's brushes for adding detail.

100mm (4in) brush

75mm (3in)

50mm (2in)

25mm (1in)

12mm (½in)

Dragging and colourwash brushes

Foam brushes

Stippling brush

Stencil brush and artist's brushes

Metal and plastic-handled radiator brushes

Paint pads

If you are new to decorating, you may find that a paint pad is easier to handle than a brush. It gives a speedy and even finish, is light to handle and works particularly well with acrylic paints. Experiment with a single pad first before investing in a kit, to make sure you are happy with the tool.

Each pad consists of a layer of fibre on top of a layer of foam, which in turn is attached to a plastic handle. Use paint pads in conjunction with a paint tray. If you purchase a kit, a tray will usually be provided.

The right roller

If speed is of the essence, a paint roller will be an indispensable part of your decorating kit. Once you have purchased a roller, you can simply buy replacement sleeves that fit the existing handle.

Use sleeves with a short pile for smooth surfaces and for applying gloss paint. Medium-pile sleeves work well on smooth and lightly-textured surfaces, and with standard and solid emulsion (latex) paint. Use long-pile sleeves on uneven and textured surfaces.

ABOVE FAR LEFT Use a cutting-in brush on a window frame.

ABOVE LEFT Load paint on to the paint pad using the tray supplied with the pad.

ABOVE Use a power roller to paint large areas.

Power rollers are mains or battery-operated and in theory they can simplify the whole process, with the paint contained in a portable reservoir. However, they can result in drips and streaks, and many professional decorators prefer more conventional methods.

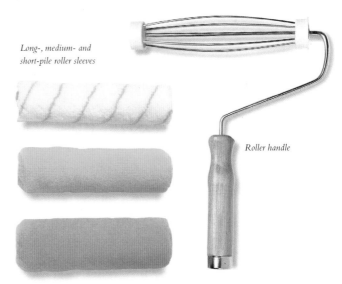

Long-, medium- and short-pile roller sleeves

Paint pads

Roller handle

Cutting-in brush

TYPES OF PAINT

Today, there are so many different shades, textures, and thicknesses of paint to choose from that making the right choice can seem bewildering. In reality, having more choice can make the job easier. Whether you are painting your house interior: kitchen, bathroom, lounge, ceiling, floor; or exterior: shed, conservatory, fences, decking, drainpipes, there is a paint to meet your needs.

DIFFERENT TYPES OF PAINT

All paints fall into one of two broad categories: water- or oil-based. Emulsion (latex) paints fit into the first category and are typically used on walls and ceilings. Oil-based paints, such as glosses and enamels, contain a solvent and they are ideal for wood surfaces such as doors, skirting (base) boards and window frames, and any metalwork. Both water- and oil-based paints come in matt (flat), mid-sheen (semi-gloss) and full gloss finishes.

If you are using emulsion paint, you will not need a separate under-coat, but you will need to apply at least two coats for good coverage. In general, gloss and enamel paints do require a separate undercoat, unless of the one-coat variety. One-coat emulsions are particularly useful when painting ceilings, reducing the amount of work involved.

Remember that if you are working with bare wood, metal, concrete or stone surfaces, you will need to apply a primer before the undercoat.

PAINT CONSISTENCY

The thickness of paint is influenced by various additives. When thinning paint make sure you use the correct diluent. At one end of the spectrum are fully-liquid paints, which require a certain amount of expertise to ensure a drip-free finish; at the other are non-drip, thixotropic or solid paints, which give a good finish whatever your skill level. Use them at cornice-level, on ceilings and above picture rails to avoid splashes.

ABOVE 1 powder pigments, 2 emulsion (latex) paints, 3 acrylic primer, 4 artist's acrylic colours, 5 acrylic scumble, 6 crackle glaze, 7 neutral wax, 8 methylated spirit (denatured alcohol), 9 brown shellac, 10 clear shellac.

BELOW FAR LEFT A selection of different-coloured paints, including watercolours, stencil paints and acrylics.

BELOW LEFT Before using, stir liquid paints with a wooden stick.

BELOW One-coat paints rapidly speed up paint decorating tasks.

SPECIAL PAINTS

Textured paints produce a relief pattern on internal walls and ceilings. They are best applied with a roller, which can be plain or have a textured patterned sleeve.

Enamel radiator paints are designed to withstand high temperatures and will not discolour like ordinary paints. You can choose from a range of bright colours to suit your decor, in satin or gloss.

Floor paints can enliven the dullest expanse of concrete, stone or wood. There is even a variety to transform tired vinyl and linoleum floors. Vary the effect with stripes, geometrical shapes or stencils for a unique look.

Kitchen and bathroom paints are specially formulated to cope with damp conditions. They contain a fungicide to stop mould growth and are considerably tougher than standard emulsions.

Microporous paints are also known as "breathing" paints. These water-based finishes, which are typically used on exterior wood, will expand

and contract with the timber. These paints also let moisture escape so you will not end up with flaky or blistered paint surfaces.

The range of special paints is growing by the day. There are paints for use on MDF (medium-density fibreboard) and melamine surfaces, plus tried and tested outdoor paints, including masonry paints for rendered surfaces, colourful garden paints for walls, containers, fences and sheds, bituminous paints for pipes and guttering, and security paints, which remain tacky to prevent would-be felons from entering the house by climbing the drainpipes.

There are also traditional paints that use authentic materials; they come in various finishes, including matt, distemper, eggshell and gloss.

ABOVE FAR LEFT Textured paints are excellent for covering minor flaws in plasterwork.

ABOVE LEFT Turn off the heating, and allow the radiator to cool before applying paint.

ABOVE Start at the innermost corner and work outward when painting floors.

PRACTICAL TIPS

• On freshly plastered walls, make sure you use a new-plaster emulsion; standard types will not allow the plaster to dry out fully.

• If the paint can you are using is still quite full, seal it, upend it to allow the paint to form a protective seal around the lid. Store the can upside down until you need it.

RIGHT Traditional, or historic, paints are the perfect choice for period houses.

FAR RIGHT Fence paints come in a wide colour range and give a weatherproof finish.

Wallpapering Equipment

Using the correct tools will make the job of hanging wallpaper much easier, allowing you to achieve a more professional finish. Some are needed specifically for wallpapering; others are likely to be part of your standard do-it-yourself tool kit. When buying decorating tools, opt for quality rather than quantity – to make sure they last longer and produce better results.

Measuring and marking

A retractable steel tape is essential for taking accurate measurements, while a long metal straightedge, a spirit level and a pencil will be needed for marking levels, vertical guidelines on walls and the positions of fixtures.

Cutting and trimming

For cutting wallpaper to length and trimming edges, you will need a pair of paperhanger's scissors, which have long blades and curved tips used for creasing paper into angles. Choose scissors that are at least 250mm (10in) long and made from stainless steel, or have been specially coated so that they will not rust.

A sharp craft knife can also be used for trimming and will be easier to use with vinyl wallcoverings. Various trimming tools are also available, including the roller cutter, which enables you to crease and cut into edges with a single movement, and is accurate and simple to use.

Pasting

For mixing and applying paste, you will need a plastic bucket and a paste brush. Proper paste brushes have synthetic bristles and will be easier to clean than ordinary paintbrushes. A pasting table is not essential, but is extremely useful. They are also inexpensive and fold for easy storage. For ready-pasted wallcoverings, a polystyrene soaking trough is required.

ABOVE A paste table is not essential, but will make the job of pasting and hanging wallcoverings much easier. Also shown are the essentials for mixing and applying paste. Keep a decorator's sponge handy to wipe away traces of adhesive on the wallcovering or paste table.

ABOVE A polystyrene trough is needed for soaking ready-pasted wallcoverings. This will allow you to carry each drop to where it will be hung, and help to keep water off the floor.

Avoiding paste drips

A length of string tied tightly across the top of a wallpaper paste bucket makes a handy brush rest. Use the string rather than the side of the bucket for removing excess adhesive from the pasting brush.

ABOVE Take accurate measurements with a retractable steel tape.

ABOVE A sharp craft knife is useful for making awkward cuts, and trimming vinyl wallcoverings.

ABOVE Use spirit levels to ensure that wallcoverings are hung straight, and pattern repeats are level.

BELOW A plumbline provides a vertical guideline for hanging the first length of wallpaper on each wall.

LEFT Paperhanger's scissors have very long blades, making it much easier to cut wallpaper neatly.

BELOW A decorator's sponge holds water well and is good for washing down walls.

BELOW A soft-bristle paperhanger's brush is the best tool for smoothing ordinary wallpaper into place.

BELOW A seam roller gives a professional finish to wallpaper seams and the edges of borders, particularly vinyl wallcoverings.

Hanging

To ensure that wallpaper is hung straight and true, a plumbline or spirit level are essential. Hanging wallpaper may also involve working at heights, so access equipment will be required. A set of sturdy steps will be suitable for papering walls, but a safe work platform will be needed for ceilings and stairwells.

Finishing

A paperhanger's brush is the best tool for smoothing down wallpaper, although a sponge can be used for vinyl wallcoverings. For the best results, choose a brush with soft, flexible bristles and buy the largest size that you can manage comfortably. Do not use wallpaper

brushes with a metal ferrule or collar on them for this job, as you might inadvertently tear or mark delicate wallcoverings.

Use a cellulose decorator's sponge rather than an ordinary household sponge. This type of sponge is made of a higher-density material, which is firmer and will hold water better. It can also be used for washing down walls before papering or painting.

A seam roller will give a neat finish to joints and the edges of borders, but should not be used on wallpaper with an embossed pattern. Various types made from wood and plastic are available. A soft plastic seam roller is the best option as it is less likely to leave marks on thin or overpasted wallpapers.

Practical tips

• A paste bucket will be easier to clean after use if it is lined with a plastic refuse sack first.

• An old flush door is a good alternative to a pasting table. Rest it between two chairs or across trestles.

• If you do not have a plumbline, improvise by using string and a large, heavy weight.

• A radiator paint roller makes an ideal tool for smoothing wallpaper in awkward corners and behind a wall fitting such as a radiator.

TYPES OF WALLCOVERING

When choosing wallcoverings, it is important to take into consideration how practical it will be in the room you wish to decorate. Each room in your home has very different requirements and by choosing the right type of wallcovering, you will be sure of a decorative surface that will wear well and look good for years to come.

LINING PAPER

This provides a smooth base for wallpaper or paint on walls and ceilings. It is made in several grades from light 480 grade, suitable for new or near perfect walls, to extra-thick 1200 grade for use on rough and pitted plaster. A good-quality lining paper will be easier to handle than a cheap, thin paper and less likely to tear when pasted.

WALLPAPERS FOR PAINTING

Woodchip paper is made by sandwiching particles of wood between two layers of paper. The thicker grades are easy to hang and cover uneven surfaces well, but woodchip is not easy to cut and can be difficult to remove, while the thinner grades tear easily. Woodchip is a budget-buy, but not particularly attractive or durable.

Relief wallpaper is imprinted with a raised, decorative surface pattern and is available in a wide choice of designs, as well as pre-cut dado (chair rail) panels and borders. It is quite easy to hang, although the thinner grades can tear when wet. It hides blemishes well and is durable once painted.

Textured vinyl has a deeply embossed surface pattern that masks

ABOVE Some wallcoverings are more hardwearing than others. Bear this in mind when choosing a pattern and material.

Lining paper

Woodchip paper

Paint-over relief wallpaper

Textured vinyl wallcovering

Heavy-duty embossed wallcovering

flaws and is uncrushable, so it is suitable for hardwearing areas such as the hall (lobby) and children's rooms. It is more expensive than relief wallpaper, but very easy to hang and usually dry strippable.

Embossed wallcovering comes in rolls and pre-cut panels made from a solid film of linseed oil and fillers fused on to a backing paper. It requires a special adhesive and will crack if folded, but it is not difficult to hang. It is very expensive, but is extremely hardwearing and durable, and the deeply-profiled, traditional designs are well suited to older and period properties.

PATTERNED WALLCOVERINGS

Printed wallpaper is available in an extensive choice of patterns and colours. The cheapest are machine-printed, but top-price designs are hand-printed and often untrimmed, so hanging is best left to the professionals. Printed wallpaper can be sponged, but is not particularly durable and is best used in rooms where it will not be subjected to much wear. The thinner grades tear easily when pasted.

Washable wallpaper also comes in a good choice of designs, but is more durable and has a thin plastic coating that allows the surface to be washed clean. It is priced competitively, fairly easy to hang and in some cases is dry strippable.

Vinyl wallcovering has a very durable surface layer of PVC that creates a hardwearing, often scrubbable, finish that resists steam, moisture and mould. There is a good choice of colours and patterns, as well as pearlized and embossed textured designs. Vinyl wallcovering is usually ready-pasted and dry strippable; paste-the-wall ranges are also available.

Sculptured vinyl is a thick, very hardwearing vinyl imprinted with a decorative design or tile effect. The waterproof finish resists steam, condensation, grease and cooking splashes, so it is a good choice for kitchens and bathrooms. It requires a heavy-duty adhesive, but is easy to hang and is dry strippable.

SPECIAL WALLCOVERINGS

Metallic foils and wallcoverings made from natural materials such as cork, silk and grasscloth can often be ordered from dedicated decorating outlets. They are expensive and difficult to hang, so employing a professional is advisable. In general, they are hard to clean, so they are best for low-wear areas of the home.

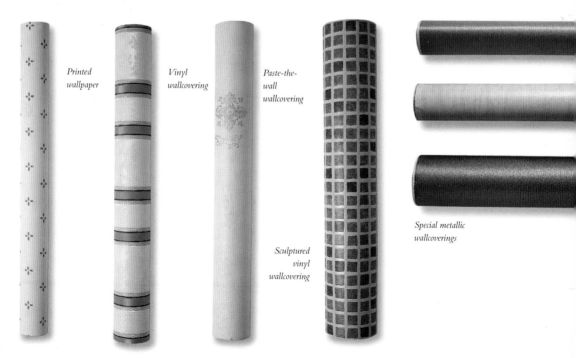

Printed wallpaper

Vinyl wallcovering

Paste-the-wall wallcovering

Sculptured vinyl wallcovering

Special metallic wallcoverings

TILING EQUIPMENT

Tiles used for wall decoration are generally fairly thin, measuring 4–6mm (³⁄₁₆–¼in) thick, although some imported tiles (especially the larger sizes) may be rather thicker than this. The commonest kinds are square, measuring 108mm (4¼in) or 150mm (6in) across, but rectangular tiles measuring 200 x 100mm (8 x 4in) and 200 x 150mm (8 x 6in) are becoming more popular.

TILING TOOLS

For almost any ceramic tiling job, large or small, a good selection of tools will simplify the whole process.

A tile file makes light work of smoothing cut edges. A tile saw is useful for making shaped cuts to fit around obstacles such as pipework. Choose the coarse variety of abrasive paper for rubbing down paintwork. An all-in-one tile cutter, or tile jig, will make life easier for a beginner. Most incorporate a measuring device, trimmer and snapping mechanism in one neat unit. A standard tile cutter works well, but requires practice for best results.

Tile spacers are required when using standard field tiles. Other types have bevelled edges that create a grouting gap automatically when butted together.

A chinagraph (wax) pencil is suitable for marking glazed surfaces such as tiles. The marks are easy to erase when the job is finished.

A notched adhesive spreader will create a series of ridges in the adhesive, allowing it to spread when the tile is pressed home and ensuring that an even thickness of adhesive is applied. A squeegee will be needed at the grouting stage to force grout into the gaps between tiles.

Additions to this basic list are a spirit level for setting out horizontal and vertical guidelines; a straight-edge and tape measure; a sponge for

cleaning off excess adhesive or applying grout; tile nippers for cutting off small pieces of tile; a glass cutter for cutting mirror tiles; a tile saw for cutting out complex shapes; and a pointing trowel for spreading adhesive on the wall. You will also need a tiling gauge for working out the positioning of tiles, made of lengths of softwood battening.

PRACTICAL TIP

• The colour of an existing tiled surface can be given a quick makeover by applying tile primer and top coat, giving you "new" tiles at a fraction of the cost.

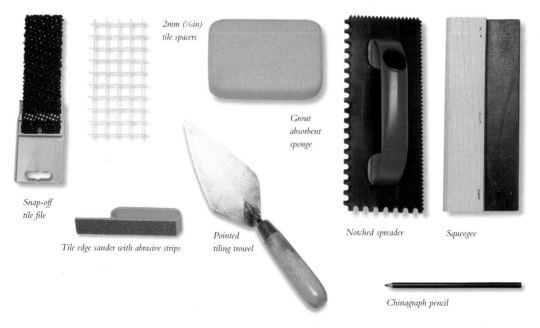

2mm (¹⁄₁₆in) tile spacers

Grout absorbent sponge

Snap-off tile file

Tile edge sander with abrasive strips

Pointed tiling trowel

Notched spreader

Squeegee

Chinagraph pencil

ADHESIVE AND GROUT

Both adhesive and grout for wall tiling are now usually sold ready-mixed in plastic tubs complete with a notched plastic spreader for your convenience. For areas that will get the occasional splash or may suffer from condensation, a water-resistant adhesive and grout is perfectly adequate, but for surfaces such as shower cubicles and around baths, which will have to withstand prolonged wetting, it is essential to use both waterproof adhesive and waterproof grout.

Always use waterproof grout on tiled worktops; ordinary grout will harbour germs. Some silicone sealant or mastic (caulking) may also be needed for waterproofing joints where tiling abuts, such as on baths, basins and shower trays.

It is important that you allow adhesive to dry for at least 24 hours before applying grout.

GROUTING

This is generally white, but coloured grout is on sale and will make a feature of the grout lines (an effect that looks best with plain or fairly neutral patterned tiles).

Adhesive and grout are both sold in a range of quantities, sometimes labelled by weight, sometimes by volume. Always check the coverage specified by the manufacturer on the packaging when buying, so as not to buy too much or run out halfway through the job.

TOOLS FOR ADHESIVE AND GROUTING

Notched spreaders are used for creating a series of ridges in the adhesive, allowing it to spread when the tile is pressed home, and ensuring that an even thickness of adhesive is applied. They are available in various sizes. Grouting tools include a grout spreader, grout finisher and grout remover.

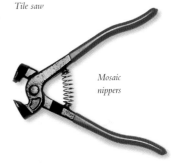

Tile saw

Mosaic nippers

Tile cutter with jaws

Grout refinishing kit

Grout remover and tile scorer (above)

Straightedge

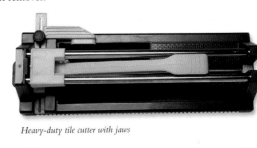

Heavy-duty tile cutter with jaws

Tile jig with adjustable width and angle facility

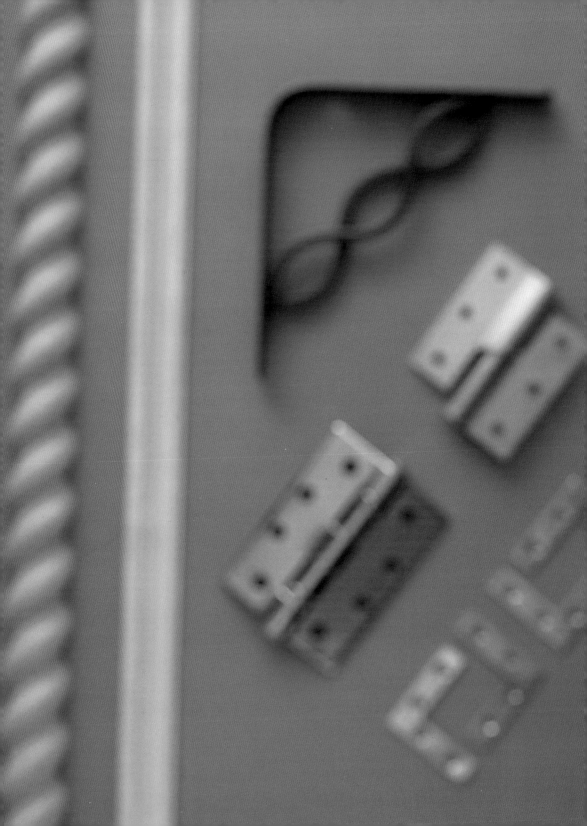

BASIC
CARPENTRY

Developing your practical skills
will allow you to tackle a wide
variety of tasks around the home –
from the simplest of jobs to the
more complex. Some basic
carpentry is involved in many
do-it-yourself jobs, such as fitting
hooks, brackets and wall bolts,
replacing cabinet doors and
drawers, and fitting shelving
systems. Once you've mastered
some basic woodworking skills,
they can be applied to a range of
repair jobs.

MAKING BASIC JOINTS

The techniques of joining wood have been developed over centuries, and there is satisfaction to be gained from employing these tried and tested methods. Patience, care and attention to detail provide the key to making accurate joints; an understanding of how they work will allow you to choose the correct type for a given job. The basic joints shown here are suitable for many projects.

DOWEL JOINTS

Beech dowels offer a quick and simple means of strengthening corner joints and aligning two components to prevent them from twisting. Three common sizes are available: 6mm (¼in), 8mm (⁵⁄₁₆in) and 10mm (⅜in). Choose the diameter to suit the material; as a general rule, do not exceed half the thickness of the timber. There are several easy methods of locating them accurately.

CENTRE-POINT METHOD

Small brass or steel centre-points that match the dowel diameter come in dowelling kits that are available from hardware stores and also include a drill bit and dowels.

MITRED JOINTS

A frame with mitred corners can be reinforced with biscuits if the parts are thick enough to accommodate them. A versatile jointing machine can save time and improve accuracy in many applications.

MAKING A DOWEL JOINT

1 Use a dowel drill bit, also called a spur-point bit, to centre each hole. A strip of tape wrapped around the bit makes a depth gauge. Hold the drill truly vertical.

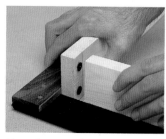
2 Insert the centre-points in the holes and push the adjacent component toward them, making sure that it is in its correct position. Use a square to check the edges are flush.

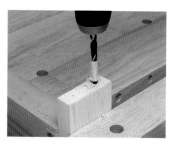
3 Clamp the second piece in a vice and drill to the correct depth for the dowel.

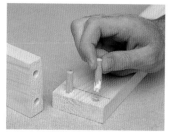
4 Apply glue to the dowels, insert in the holes and tap the joint together.

MAKING A MITRED JOINT WITH BISCUITS

1 A mitre saw will cut through the timber easily and accurately.

2 Use a try or combination square to align the corners accurately when marking.

3 The oval shape of the biscuit automatically centres the mitred joint as it fits together.

JOINING BOARDS AND KNOCK-DOWN FITTINGS

Manufactured sheet materials are available in large sizes, but occasionally it is necessary to join them together neatly. Because they lend themselves to machine-made joints, there are several options to choose from. Knock-down (K-D) fittings are used extensively in the furniture industry for manufacturing self-assembly units. They are useful for furniture that needs to be reassembled easily.

LAP JOINT

A lap joint is easily made with a router machine and is useful when matching veneered boards to make decorative panels.

LOOSE-TONGUED JOINT

An even stronger bond can be achieved by using a "loose tongue", which acts as a key for the adhesive. This type of joint takes little time to fabricate.

SCARF JOINT

Two panels can be joined with a feather-edged scarf joint, which will provide a large surface area for the glue. When made correctly, this type of joint will allow the completed panel to be formed into a curve without the joint separating or kinking.

> ### PRACTICAL TIP
>
> • Use special construction screws when joining chipboard (particle board) panels. They have a coarse thread designed to grip the fibres in the panels without splitting them.

MAKING A LAP JOINT

1 Use a router fitted with a fence to form the lap, cutting it to exactly half the thickness of the material.

2 Apply glue and clamp the boards together. When the veneers are well matched, the seam will be almost invisible to the eye.

MAKING A LOOSE-TONGUED JOINT

1 Use 6mm (¼in) plywood for a loose tongue. The cross-ply structure is stronger than a long-grained section of hardwood. Apply glue and insert into a routed groove.

2 Firmly clamp the two panels flat to the bench before applying longitudinal pressure to the joint. This will keep it perfectly flat and produce a strong bond.

MAKING A SCARF JOINT

1 This straightforward joint can be made easily with hand tools. Make up a simple wooden jig on the workbench to control the angle of the plane.

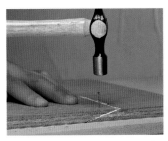

2 Before clamping the joint together, drive in a few panel pins (brads) to prevent the boards from sliding around. Remove them when the glue has dried.

FITTING LIGHTWEIGHT FIXTURES

Installing new fixtures and fittings is a basic do-it-yourself activity that covers a variety of tasks, such as hanging a picture, fitting drawer and door handles, putting up lightweight shelving, and fitting hooks, locks, clasps and catches on all manner of items. Many are very straightforward jobs, which involve simply screwing, pinning or sticking the fixture in place.

SUPPORTING LIGHTWEIGHT HOOKS AND SHELVING

Fixtures of this kind include coat hooks, cup hooks and dozens of other quickly fitted aids and clips of all types. Threaded hooks and eyes need a pilot hole to be made with a bradawl, after which they can be screwed in place with finger and thumb. Small shelves can be supported in a variety of ways, including using screw eyes, dowels and lengths of wood. All these methods are suitable for shelving that will carry little weight.

FIXING HANGING RAILS TO WALLS

When attaching a clothes or towel rail to a plaster or plasterboard (gypsum board) wall, it is best to fix a small wooden block to the wall at each end, using a single, central screw, then screw the rail brackets to the blocks.

This avoids the need to drill closely-spaced holes in the wall for the fixing plates, which could cause the surface to crumble, or for the holes to merge into each other.

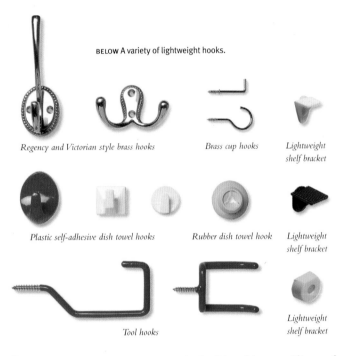

BELOW A variety of lightweight hooks.

Regency and Victorian style brass hooks

Brass cup hooks

Lightweight shelf bracket

Plastic self-adhesive dish towel hooks

Rubber dish towel hook

Lightweight shelf bracket

Tool hooks

Lightweight shelf bracket

HANGING A CABINET

A good way to hang a small cabinet is with a wooden batten (furring strip) fixed to the wall with screws and plugs. The tapered top edge of the rail engages with a recess in the back of the cabinet, providing a safe mounting, yet allowing the cabinet to be lifted down when required. It is essential to ensure that the angles of both nails are the same for a good and secure fitting.

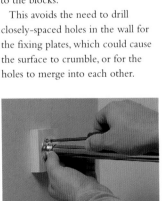

ABOVE When fixing hanging rails, insert a wooden block between the fitting and the wall.

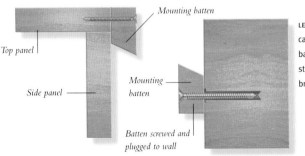

Top panel

Mounting batten

Side panel

Mounting batten

Batten screwed and plugged to wall

LEFT Hanging cabinets with battens into studwork or brickwork.

Hanging a Picture

When hanging any artwork, it is important to consider the weight and size of the frame. Use picture wire or strong cord to hang any weight of frame. Light pictures can be hung with a single picture hook, which incorporates a hardened pin rather like a masonry nail and is driven directly into the wall. Single or double D-rings are strong fixings for light to medium-weight frames, but you should use strap hangers for heavy or large frames. These are screwed on to the back section of the frame and wire or cord can be attached in the same way. However, if the frame is very heavy, it is recommended to hang the picture from the loops of the strap hanger on to screws inserted directly into the wall. Anti-theft devices (ATDs) and mirror plates work in much the same way as strap hangers. The straight section is screwed into the back of the frame, and the curved section is screwed to the wall.

Setting a striking plate (keeper) for a door catch

Fitting a striking plate incorporates the tasks likely to be encountered in the fixing of many small fittings: accurate positioning and marking, skill in cutting recesses to different

LEFT 1 Picture wire
2 Mirror plates
3 Anti-theft devices
4 Screws
5 Rivets or butterflies
6 Strap hangers
7 Spring clips
8 Picture cord
9 Double D-rings
10 Single D-rings

depths, and the accurate fitting of countersunk screws. You should offer the striking plate to the timber, making sure that it is in the correct position and square with both the lock and the door frame. Scribe around it, including the hole in the centre. Carefully chisel along the marked outline, starting with the cut across the grain at each end. Then chisel out the waste to the depth of the plate. You will need to cut deeper with the chisel to create the mortise for the catch. Hold the plate in position and use a bradawl or gimlet to prick the positions of the screw holes. Drive in the screws, making sure that they fit flush into the countersunk holes in the plate.

Surface-mounted catches

The roller catch is often used on small cabinet doors, especially those in a kitchen. Offer up the striking plate first, marking the screw positions, drilling pilot holes and screwing the plate to the frame. Both striking plate and roller have elongated holes to allow for adjustment. The roller is fitted in the same way and adjusted accordingly.

The magnetic catch is also common. This is even simpler to fix, since it can be placed in a variety of positions on the door. Large doors may be fitted with two catches, one top and one bottom. Slotted mounting holes allow adjustment so that the catch works efficiently.

ABOVE A striking plate set in an internal frame.

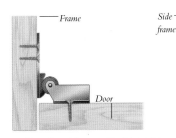

Frame

Door

ABOVE Use roller catches on cabinet doors for a smooth opening action.

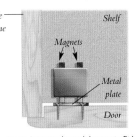

Side frame

Shelf

Magnets

Metal plate

Door

ABOVE A magnetic catch is easy to fit but you may need to use more than one on large doors.

FITTING HEAVYWEIGHT FIXTURES

Heavyweight fixtures around the home tend to be of a permanent nature. Items such as sturdy shelving for books, and cabinets, wall-mounted televisions and cabinet speakers are very heavy, need a lot of support and tend to remain where they are installed originally. For this reason, heavy wall fixings are designed to be permanent.

OBTAINING A GOOD FIXING

A frequently encountered problem with heavy fixtures is obtaining a good fixing in masonry. A traditional method, which is quite acceptable, is to drill and plug a wall with home-made tapered wooden plugs, driven in hard, and then screw into them.

There are some useful commercial products, too, such as the rawl bolt, which expands inside the hole as it is tightened and will provide a secure fixing for heavy shelving or wall units.

Post anchors are another option, although they are designed mainly for vertical posts outdoors. Some are adjustable to take either 75 or 100mm (3 or 4in) posts and can be used horizontally to fix the frames

for stud (dry) walling to concrete or stonework. Hanger screws are an easy method of fixing into woodwork to leave projecting studding, which can be used to secure heavy bookcases and room dividers, yet allow them to be removed simply by undoing the nuts.

ANGLE BRACKETS

Many sizes of angle and straight steel bracket are available, and they have a variety of uses. Among them are fixing the top and bottom frames for wardrobes. They should be fitted inside the framing so that they cannot be seen. The top brackets should be screwed into the ceiling joists, which you might have to locate by prodding with a sharp tool

through the plaster, while the floor brackets should be screwed directly to the floorboards. Much the same applies to fitting the sliding rails for the doors.

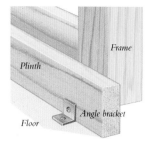

The expanded wall bolt grips the masonry

Tighten nut   *Screw thread*

ABOVE How to fix a wall bolt.

Rawl bolt: used with studding

Rawl bolt: standard wall bolt

BELOW A selection of heavy-duty wall bolts.

Rawl hook

Rawl eye

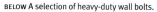

Ceiling   *Angle brackets*

Frame

Wall

Frame

Plinth

Floor   *Angle bracket*

ABOVE Angle brackets positioned as above ensure stability and squareness.

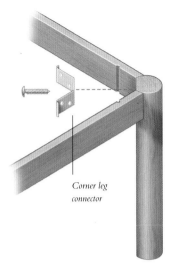

Corner leg connector

ABOVE Steel angle plates or brackets, or knock-down fittings, can be used to strengthen joints, as well as allowing a piece of furniture to be taken apart if required. These ingenious corner brackets are used to fix the detachable legs and connect the side rails at the same time.

HEAVY-DUTY BRACKETS

There are many heavy-duty brackets to choose from, making all manner of joints possible. One of the most frequently used in the home is the joist hanger. This may be nailed or screwed to an existing timber beam to carry flooring joists, very heavy shelving or similar constructions. Some joist hangers are designed to lip into brickwork. Simple angled plates can be used for bracing the frames of stud walls. They may be nailed or screwed in place. You can also buy heavy-duty fixings for putting up bicycles, racks and ladders in garages. Most are simply bent angle irons with pre-drilled holes.

FITTING A TELEVISION SHELF

In a small room, a television is best mounted in a corner, otherwise it will have to be fixed high on the wall, which will make viewing difficult. When installing a television

ABOVE A heavy steel bracket can be used for bracing a frame joint.

(or microwave) shelf, always follow the manufacturer's instructions, but generally you should offer the backplate to the wall at the desired height, making sure the television can swing around to the angle required, and mark its position. Drill holes for the bolts, screw them into place and add the movable shelf. Position the television and arrange the wiring so that it will not tangle.

Steel angle brackets are usually pre-drilled

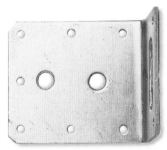

Heavy brackets (above and below) with multiple fixing options

BELOW A selection of heavy-duty brackets.

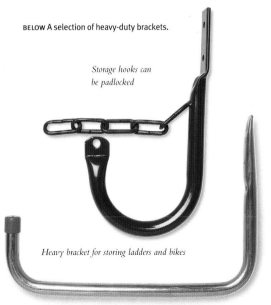

Storage hooks can be padlocked

Heavy bracket for storing ladders and bikes

FITTING SHELVES

Putting up shelves is a fundamental do-it-yourself task, and is probably one of the first jobs the newcomer will tackle. With a little thought, shelving can be made to be decorative as well as functional, and a variety of materials, including wood, metal and glass, can be used to good effect. All require firm wall fixings and always use a spirit level when fitting shelves.

SIMPLE SHELVING

Ready-made shelving systems can be employed, both wall-mounted and freestanding. The basic methods of fitting shelving are the same, no matter what material is used. Essential requirements are establishing a truly level surface with a spirit level, obtaining firm fixings in the wall, and being able to fit accurately into an alcove.

Use your spirit level to ascertain the height and horizontal run of the shelf, then mark the positions for the brackets. Mark the positions of the screws through the holes in the brackets, drill with a masonry bit and insert wallplugs. Hold each bracket in place and start all the screws into the wallplugs before tightening them fully. This will ensure that they engage properly.

If fitting more than one shelf on an uninterrupted run of wall, mark them out at the same time, using a try or combination square. Cut them to size, then screw them to the shelf brackets.

A variety of simple shelf brackets

Decorative steel bracket

Decorative brass bracket

A variety of very lightweight plastic shelf fittings

FITTING A SIMPLE SHELF

1 Mark the position of the shelf with a level placed on top of a batten (furring strip).

2 Mark the position of the screws through the bracket holes.

3 Drill and insert your plugs. Start all the screws before tightening up.

4 Screw up the bracket into the shelf to make a secure fixing.

5 You can also attach the shelf to the brackets before mounting the brackets to the wall.

1 Use two battens (furring strips) clamped together to measure in a confined space.

2 Transfer the measurement on to the wood to be used for the shelf and cut to length.

3 Align the position and fit the rear shelf using a spirit level and screw in position.

ALCOVES

An easy way to measure the internal width of an alcove is by using two overlapping strips. Allow them to touch each end of the alcove and clamp them together on the overlap. Transfer this measurement to the shelving material and carefully cut it to length.

Establish the position for the back batten with a spirit level. Drill and plug the holes, then screw the batten in place. Using the back batten as a reference point, fit the side battens to the end walls of the alcove.

Drill screw clearance holes in the shelf, place the shelf on the battens and screw it down. When fitting shelves into an alcove, do not cut all the shelves to the same size. If the sides of the alcove are plasterwork, brick or stone, there will almost certainly be some discrepancies in the width from top to bottom, so measure for each shelf individually and cut them separately.

If there is an uneven gap along the back of a shelf, caused by an uneven wall surface, you can hide the gap by pinning quadrant moulding (a base shoe) along the back edge of the shelf.

4 Drill the holes in the side battens and screw into place using the back batten as a guide.

5 Pre-drill the screw holes in the shelf and screw on to the side battens from the top.

PLANNING SHELVES

Think of how to make best use of the new storage space. Make a rough sketch of the plans, in order to take into account which items are going to be stored, such as the height and width of books, or the clearance that ornaments and photographs require. Aim to keep everyday items within easy reach, which in practice is between about 750mm (2ft 6in) and 1.5m (5ft) above the floor. Position deep shelves near the bottom so that it is easy to see and reach the back. Allow 25–50mm (1–2in) of clearance on top of the height of the objects to be stored, so that they are easy to take down and put back.

Think about weight too. If the shelves are going to store heavy objects, the shelving material must be chosen with care, since thin shelves will sag if heavily loaded unless they are well supported. With 12mm (½in) chipboard (particle board) and ready-made veneered or melamine-faced shelves, space brackets at 450mm (18in) for heavy loads or 600mm (2ft) for light loads. With 19mm (¾in) chipboard or 12mm (½in) plywood, increase the spacing to 600mm (2ft) and 750mm (2ft 6in) respectively. For 19mm (¾in) plywood, blockboard, MDF (medium-density fibreboard) or natural wood, the bracket spacing can be 750mm (2ft 6in) for heavy loads, 900mm (3ft) for light ones.

FITTING SHELVING SYSTEMS

Storage can be provided in one of two ways. One is to buy or make pieces of freestanding furniture that match the required storage function. The other is to use raw materials such as wood and manufactured boards plus the appropriate hardware to create built-in storage space, arrays of shelving, closets in alcoves, wardrobes and so on.

BUYING SHELVING SYSTEMS

Shelving systems abound in do-it-yourself stores for those who prefer simply to fit rather than to make the shelving. There is a range of brackets on the market to cater for every need, and these clip into slotted uprights screwed to the wall. The bracket positions can be adjusted to vary the spacing between the shelves to accommodate your needs.

Shelving systems are a versatile way of dealing with changing requirements, and they have the distinct advantage of being portable when you need to move them. They are capable of holding heavy weights, but remember that ultimately a shelf's capacity depends on the strength of the wall fixing employed.

First measure the distance between the shelving uprights, bearing in mind the thickness and material to be used for the shelf. Books can be very heavy, so do not set the uprights too far apart, otherwise the shelf will sag in the middle. About a quarter of the length of the shelf can overhang each end. If necessary, cut the uprights to length. Drill and plug the wall so that you can attach one upright by its topmost hole. Do not tighten the screw fully at this stage. Simply allow the upright to hang freely.

Hold your spirit level against the side of the upright, and when you are satisfied that it is vertical, mark its position lightly on the wall with a pencil. Mark in the remaining screw positions, then drill and plug the rest of the screw holes.

FITTING A SHELVING SYSTEM

1 Measure the distance between the uprights. Do not set the brackets too far apart.

2 Fix the first screw loosely and let the upright hang.

3 Check the bracket is absolutely vertical with a spirit level.

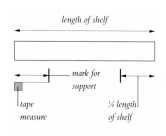

4 A little packing card may be necessary if the wall is uneven.

5 Mark the position for the second upright using the first as a guide.

6 The shelf brackets can be inserted at different heights and can be easily moved.

You may find that when you tighten the screws, the upright needs a little packing here and there to keep it vertical in the other plane. If these discrepancies are not too large, this adjustment can be done by varying the relative tightness of the screws, which will pull the upright into line. You can mark off the position for the second upright and any others, using a spirit level on top of a shelf with a couple of brackets slipped into position. Fitting the second upright entails the same procedure as before.

ABOVE A well-organized shelving arrangement for a wardrobe system.

FREESTANDING SHELVING

These shelving units usually come packed flat for home assembly. They can be very useful and versatile pieces of furniture. They are available in a variety of materials, including pine, manufactured boards and metal. Knock-down joints are often used in their construction.

There is a possibility that boisterous children could pull freestanding shelving over, so it is worth attaching a unit to a wall, if only temporarily until the children are a little older. This can be done with a couple of brackets screwed and plugged to the wall, or with brackets to the floor.

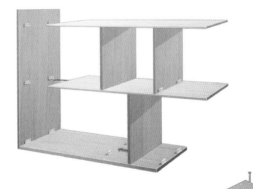

LEFT Knock-down joints are used primarily in symmetrical structures to ensure squareness.

PRACTICAL TIPS

• If there is a gap along the back of a shelf, caused by an uneven wall, you can hide the gap by pinning quadrant moulding (a base shoe) along the back edge of the shelf.

• Select screw sizes according to the load that a shelf will take.

CORNER UNITS

A popular form of shelving, corner units represent an efficient way of using what otherwise might be redundant space. They can be made from plywood with some form of lipping applied to the front edge to hide the laminations, or they can be quite ornate and made in an expensive hardwood. Cut the triangular shelves so that the angle at the apex, which fits into the corner, is slightly over 90 degrees. This will ensure that the front edges touch the wall where they will be seen. Mirror plates provide a neat, unobtrusive means of fixing corner units.

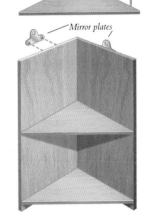

Mirror plates

ABOVE Mirror plates hang the cabinet rather than pinning it to the wall.

HANGING DOORS

Installing a new door is not a difficult task, but the job does need patience, precision and organization to go smoothly. A methodical step-by-step approach will pay off. The following sequence relates to hanging a new door, and you may only need to trim some of the door. When finished, check that the door swings freely and closes properly without catching the frame.

TYPES OF DOOR

Many modern internal doors are hollow structures with "egg-box" centres and solid timber lippings around the edges. They offer little flexibility for trimming to fit frames that are out of square, which often occurs in an old building. For this reason, as well as for aesthetic appeal, use only solid doors in older houses.

PUTTING IN A NEW DOOR

Measure the frame accurately, top to bottom and side to side, then choose a door that will fit as closely as possible. Even so, it will probably need to be cut to fit.

Joggles, or horns, may project from the ends of the door to protect it in transit. Mark these off level with the top of the door, using a try square.

Place the door on a flat surface and carefully cut the joggles flush with the ends of the door, using a hand saw. Offer up the door to the frame, placing wedges underneath (chisels are handy) to raise it off the floor by about 12mm (½in) to allow for a carpet or other floorcovering.

Mark the door in pencil while it is wedged in place to allow for a 3mm

HANGING A DOOR

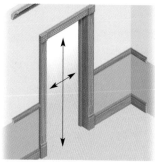

1 Measure the door frame to assess the size of the door you require.

2 If there are joggles, square them off accurately using a try or combination square.

3 Remove the joggles with a hand saw making a clean, square cut.

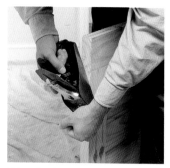

7 Plane the edges, working in from both sides. Offer the door into the frame to check it fits.

8 Lay the hinge on the door and cut around it with a sharp knife.

9 Alternatively, scribe the outline of the hinge on to the door with a marking gauge.

(⅛in) clearance at the top and sides. Place the door back on the flat surface and saw off the bulk of the waste, leaving the marked lines still visible. Plane down the sides of the door to the marked lines, working with the grain, then plane the top, working in from each side to avoid splintering the wood. Replace the door in the frame, wedging it once more to hold it. If you are satisfied with the fit, you can hang it.

Hold each hinge in position, about 150mm (6in) from the top and 225mm (9in) from the bottom of the door, with the knuckle projecting just beyond the face of the door; mark it with a knife. For a heavy door, a third hinge will be needed, positioned centrally between the other two. Working around the marked outline, cut vertically down into the wood to the depth of the hinge flap with a chisel.

Make a series of cuts across the width of the recess, to the same depth, and remove the waste with a chisel. Place the hinge in the recess, drill small pilot holes for the screws, but fit only one screw at this stage. Repeat with the other hinge.

Open the hinges and offer the hinge side of the door to the frame, placing wedges under it to raise it to the correct height. Press the free flap of each hinge against the frame and mark around it in pencil. Cut the recesses. Drill pilot holes and hang the door, again fitting only one screw in each hinge flap. When you are satisfied with the fit and operation of the door, insert all the screws, making sure that the heads lie flat in the countersinks of the hinges, otherwise the door will not close properly.

PRACTICAL TIP

• When hanging a door, you'll need someone to help with positioning.

4 Offer the door into the frame. Use a wedge to square up if need be.

5 Mark the clearance on to the frame using a pencil and a 3mm (⅛in) washer as a guide.

6 Saw off the bulk of the waste using your knee as a support on the end of the door.

10 Chop out the waste with a sharp chisel working along the scribed line.

11 Insert the hinge into the recess and screw up tightly.

12 Mark the other part of the hinge on to the door frame with a pencil.

REPLACING CABINET DOORS AND DRAWERS

Old and tired-looking cabinets can often be revived by a coat of paint, the addition of stencilled patterns or the application of decorative laminates, however, sometimes the only way to revive them is to renew the doors and drawer fronts themselves. This is neither a complex nor very expensive job and it can be fun to do.

REPLACING CHIPBOARD DOORS

This may also be necessary if the hinges have failed in chipboard doors, which can occur with kitchen furniture after a number of years because of its heavy workload. If you replace old chipboard doors with new ones, they must be exactly the same size and be hung in the same way as the originals, since they cannot be trimmed to fit. Doors such as these are readily available, along with the chipboard hinges necessary to fit them. It is important to ensure that the hinge positions are perfectly accurate and that their recesses are of the correct depth, so careful measuring and a reliable drill stand or pillar drill is essential.

Remove the old door from the hinge baseplates by slackening each retaining screw, not the adjuster, and sliding the door off. Then release the two retaining screws and remove each hinge from the door, leaving a circular hole.

Place the new door over the old one so that the top edges are aligned, then measure down to the centre of each hole. Next measure to the centre of each hole from the edge to locate their positions exactly.

ABOVE Revive tired-looking kitchen cabinets with a new coat of paint or new doors.

Use a combination square as a gauge to take the centre position from the old door and transfer it to the new one. Mark the positions of the hinge holes on the new door with a centre punch. Bore the hinge recesses with a pillar drill or a drill mounted in a drill stand for accuracy. Be sure to set the stop to the correct depth.

Insert the hinges, making sure they are square to the edge of the door and screw them in place. Replace the door, using the adjustment screws to obtain a perfect fit with the face of the unit.

REPLACING A DOOR

1 Take off the old hinge simply by unscrewing it from the side.

2 Measure accurately from the edge of the old door to the hinge hole.

3 Transfer the mark to the new door to ensure a perfect position for the new hinge.

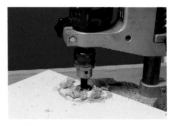

4 Drill out a new hole, preferably using a static drill stand for accuracy.

5 Attach the new hinge in the same position on the new door as the old.

1 Remove the old drawer front by unscrewing it from behind.

2 Drill the new front using the existing holes as a guide.

3 Screw the new drawer front into position from behind.

DRAWER FRONTS

The drawers of modern furniture are often made with false fronts that allow a basic carcass to be used in a number of different styles. To replace, open the drawer or, better still, remove it completely. From inside the drawer, slacken the screws holding the false front to the carcass and remove it. Place the old front over the new one, aligning it exactly, drill down through the screw holes and into the new front to make pilot holes for the screws. Take care not to drill right through the new face and spoil the finish. Use a depth stop to prevent this. Finally, screw the new front to the carcass from the inside.

PRACTICAL TIP

- When fitting screws in hardwood doors, always drill pilot holes for them, otherwise it may be impossible to drive them in completely. Brass or small gauge screws may even snap.

FITTING A LOUVRE DOOR

1 Fit a flush hinge to the door. Surface mounting makes this easy.

2 Screw a magnetic catch beneath the bottom shelf of the cabinet.

3 Screw a magnetic catchplate to the door, both the top and bottom.

4 Change the handle or knob to suit the style of your door.

FITTING SOLID WOOD DOORS

With solid-timber-framed cabinets, an attractive option is to fit louvred doors, which are made of solid timber and are available in a host of standard sizes.

Fitting louvre doors, or other solid wooden doors, to cabinets follows the basic procedures for hanging any door. First fit the hinges to the inside of the door, then open the hinges and fit them to the cabinet stile. Note that fitting a cabinet door with butt hinges is only recommended for solid timber framing.

Cabinet doors can be fitted with a variety of handles and knobs to suit the style of furniture. Often, changing the handles alone can improve the appearance of a cabinet considerably. A small brass handle, for example, makes a nice finish or use stainless steel for a modern look.

REPLACING WALL-MOUNTED BOARDS

Skirting (base) boards receive a lot of wear and tear from scuffing by feet and furniture, which is why they are there in the first place, of course. From time to time, the damage may be so great, such as after replacing flooring, including woodstrip or laminate flooring, that sections of skirting or even complete lengths of it need to be replaced.

TYPES OF BOARDS

Skirting boards may vary from simple rectangular sections of timber to quite ornate moulded profiles. Similarly, picture rails and dado rails, sometimes called chair rails because they protect the walls from damage by chair backs, may need to be renewed or repaired. In many ways these tasks are similar.

DEALING WITH CORNERS

When fitting a moulded shape with concave curves into a corner, the correct way to achieve the joint is to scribe it. This is done by marking the profile of one board on to the back of the other with the aid of a small offcut of the moulding. Then a coping saw is used to cut along the marked line, allowing the board to fit neatly over its neighbour. This technique avoids the mismatch of ends that can occur when some mouldings are mitred at 45 degrees, using a mitre box or mitre saw. However, to cut an external mitre for a wall return, use a mitre saw or mitre box in the normal way.

SKIRTING BOARD

In a rectangular room, it is always best to fit the two long sections of skirting board first and then fit the shorter ones to them. It makes handling, lifting and fixing much

PRACTICAL TIP

• Many skirting boards are fixed with flooring, or cut-nails, which are square-edged and grip extremely well. Almost certainly they will split a small section of replacement skirting, so use masonry nails instead and drill pilot holes in the skirting.

easier. To fit the boards, first prise the old board partially away from the wall, using a crowbar (wrecking bar), then insert wedges to hold it far enough away to allow you to get at it with a saw. Place a mitre block

REPLACING A SECTION OF SKIRTING BOARD

1 Prise away the old skirting board with a crowbar (wrecking bar) and a wedge.

2 Cut away the damaged section with a mitre box and a saw.

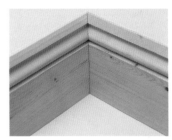

3 Mark each end of the new section of board and mitre the ends.

4 Hammer nails into the new section of board while holding a plank against the wood.

ABOVE Internal and external mitres of a skirting board.

1 Prise away the old rail from the wall using a crowbar.

2 Remove any residual nails in the wall or plaster with a pair of pincers.

3 Fill any cracks or holes in the plasterwork with filler.

tight against the board and, with a tenon saw, nibble away at it at 45 degrees until the board is cut in half. Repeat the 45-degree cut at the other end of the section to be replaced and remove the length of old skirting. Then offer up the replacement section, mark each end with a pencil and mitre accordingly.

A good way to hold the new section in position is to lay a plank so that it butts up against the skirting and kneel on it while driving the nails home.

REPLACING A PICTURE OR DADO (CHAIR) RAIL

Use a crowbar to prise the old picture rail away from the wall, inserting a block of wood under its head to protect the plaster and to give extra leverage.

Remove any nails that remain in the wall with a pair of pincers, again using a block of wood to protect the wall. Make good the nail holes with filler, leaving it slightly proud at this stage. When the filler is completely dry, sand it down with abrasive paper wrapped around a cork block or

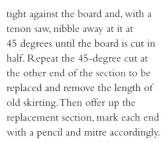

4 Sand off the dry filler with abrasive paper to get a smooth finish.

block of wood to give a perfectly flat, smooth surface. Fit the new picture rail, scribing or mitring the ends as necessary.

FIXING METHODS

Cut-nails, such as those used to fix skirting boards, have long been used to fix picture rails, Delft rails and the like, but you may find that they are not available in your local store. Any ordinary wire lost-head nail is a good alternative when fixing through plasterwork into stud (dry) walling, as long as you know where the studs are.

5 Fit the new rail to the wall, making sure it is properly level.

CUTTING A SCRIBED JOINT

Use a scrap of the board as a guide. Grip a pencil against the scrap of wood and run it down the surface of the back of the board to transfer the outline. Cut it out with a coping saw.

GLOSSARY

Architrave (trim) A type of timber moulding, used mainly around openings in walls for doors.

Batten (furring strip) A name given to a straight length of timber, used for temporary or permanent support e.g. of roof tiles, wall tiles or for setting concrete.

Bevel An angled edge on, for example, a piece of wood. Also see *chamfer*. Also a carpenter's tool for setting an angle.

Building regulations Legal requirements in the UK and other countries for the ways that houses are constructed (and modified).

Butt joint A joint between two pieces of timber when one piece simply meets the other, such as in an L-shape or a T-shape or end-to-end.

Caulking gun A device for squeezing sealant or adhesive out of a cartridge.

Centre point The sharp point of a *twist drill bit* or a metal plug put into a *dowel* hole to transfer its position to a second piece of wood.

Chamfer An angled edge to timber, usually smaller than a *bevel*.

Chipboard (particle board) An inexpensive manufactured board consisting of timber scraps and glue.

Clearance hole A hole drilled to take the full size of a screw.

Consumer unit The modern term for an electrical fuse-box. It may contain miniature circuit breakers rather than fuses depending on its age.

Combination ladder A ladder that can be used in two or more ways. Uses include: step-ladder, straight ladder, stair ladder and extending ladder.

Cornice, Cove (crown molding) A decorative timber, plaster or polystyrene (styrofoam) moulding to cover up the join between wall and ceiling.

Counterbore To enlarge a hole, e.g. to take a bolt or screw head.

Countersink An angled recess to take the head of a countersunk screw. Also tool for making the same.

Depth stop A device attached to an electric drill to limit the depth of a hole being drilled.

Door furniture A general term for the bits screwed on to doors, such as handles, knockers and knobs.

Dovetail A woodworking joint, where angled pins in one piece of wood fit into identical angled recesses in the other. Also describes fine-toothed backsaw used for making same.

Dowel A circular timber peg used for reinforcing woodworking joints.

End grain The fibres at the end of a piece of wood that are highly absorbent.

Fascia (board) The vertical timber boards at the eaves. Gutters are usually fixed to these.

Flashing Strips cut from lead or zinc sheet used to seal roofing junctions.

Former A word for a mould around which something else shapes itself.

Fused connection unit An electrical fitting allowing electric equipment to be permanently wired in.

Gable The pointed walls, sometimes found at the ends of a pitched roof.

Gloss paint An oil-based paint with a shiny finish used on wood and metal.

Grain The texture of timber created by the annual growth of a tree.

Handed Refers to hinges (e.g. rising butt hinges) attached to either the right or the left of the door.

Housing (also housing joint) A woodworking joint where one piece of wood fits into a slot (housing) in another piece.

Jamb Vertical timbers that form the sides of window and door frames.

Knot A dark coloured circle in wood where a branch grew out of the tree. It can exude resin or can fall out.

Lath-and-plaster An old-fashioned way of constructing ceilings and partition walls. The plaster is applied to thin timber strips (laths), which are secured to vertical studs (walls) or horizontal joists (ceilings).

Lipping A thin strip (often of hardwood) applied to the edges of a timber board (e.g. a shelf or a countertop).

Mastic (caulking) A non-setting and flexible waterproof sealant.

MDF Medium-density fibreboard. A manufactured board consisting of timber fibres and resin. Has smooth surface and will take screws and nails, but needs handling with care.

Melamine An easy-to-clean plastic often used for covering *chipboard* (particle board) to make shelving boards.

Mitre A joint made by cutting two pieces of wood at 45 degrees, such as for making picture frames.

Mitre fence A platform on a fixed sander to support mouldings while the mitred end is sanded.

Mortise A deep slot cut in timber, for example, for a mortise lock. A mortise chisel is a strong type for levering out the wood. See also *tenon*.

Oilstone A flat abrasive stone used with oil for sharpening chisels and knives.

Party wall The wall between two semi-detached houses or two terraced houses.

Pilot hole A small hole drilled to guide a larger drill or to take the point of a screw that then cuts its own thread.

Plasterboard (gypsum board) Sheets consisting of solid plaster contained by heavy paper sheets, used for constructing partition walls and ceilings.

Plywood A man-made board consisting of thin sheets glued together. Alternate sheets have the grain running at right angles giving it exceptional strength.

Pointing Using extra mortar to finish the joints between bricks in a wall.

Punched Applied to nail heads to mean that they are pushed below the surface of timber with a nail punch.

PVA (white) glue Strictly polyvinyl acetate: a type of adhesive used for wood-working, also used in concreting work to reduce the absorbency of surfaces.

Rafters Sloping timber members of a roof.

Rebate (rabbet) A slot cut out of the corner of timber to hold something.

Render A mixture of sand and cement used to coat external walls.

Residual current device An electrical safety device that prevents electric shock.

Reveal The rectangular hole in a wall in which a window or door is fitted.

Rim lock (rim latch) A lock (or latch) that is attached to the surface of a door unlike a *mortise* lock, which fits into a slot cut out of the door.

Rising butts Hinges that lift a door as it is opened.

Router An electrical woodworking tool that cuts a slot or a recess.

Sash A name for a window, usually applied to sash windows where each window slides vertically.

Screed A thin layer of sand and cement applied to concrete floors.

Set The way in which alternate teeth on a hand saw are bent away from the blade to make the cut wider than the saw blade and so prevent the saw from sticking.

Shuttering A framework of timber boards used to hold concrete while it sets.

Silicone A flexible non-setting plastic used in sealants.

Skew (toe) nailing Driving nails in at an angle to provide a stronger bond.

Soffit The horizontal timber boards used at the eaves.

Soil pipe The large vertical drainage pipe in houses taking the toilet waste.

Spigot A projection designed to fit into a recess.

Stile The vertical timber pieces of a door or window.

Stopcocks Valves fitted to water pipes to stop the flow of water through them.

Stopping A filler for use with wood.

Stud A vertical timber strut used for internal partition walls.

Tamping Using something heavy to compact materials.

Template A guide for drilling or cutting.

Tenon A reduced section on one piece of wood designed to fit into a slot (*mortise*) in another.

Tongued-and-grooved A method of joining planks (such as floorboards or cladding) edge to edge – a tongue on one piece fits into a groove in its neighbour.

Trap A device fitted in the waste pipe under a bath, basin or sink to prevent foul air and small animals getting in.

Twist drill bits Drills for making holes in wood and metal.

Veneer A very thin layer of expensive timber attached to a cheaper base.

Waste Any piece of material that is cut off and not used.

Waste pipe The pipe taking dirty water from bath, basins, sinks and showers.

ACKNOWLEDGEMENTS

PICTURE CREDITS
The publisher would like to thank the following agencies, individuals and companies for the permission to reproduce the following images.

Axminster Power Tool Centre: 11bc; 12tc; 16r; 28br; 33tc; 34c; 37br; 43c. **DIY Photo Library**: 45 steps 1–5; 56tr. **John Freeman**: 76–7. **Simon Gilham**: 50bc. **HSS Tool Hire**: 12c; 13t, c, r; 49br. **Hunter Plastics** 52–3. **Mr. Mark Blewitt**: 50tr.

The publisher would like to thank the following individuals and companies for their help with photography and images:

Axminster Power Tool Centre

Burlington Slate Limited
Cavendish House
Kirkby-in-Furness
Cumbria
LA17 7UN
Tel: 01229 889661

Dewalt Power Tools

Eternit Building Materials

Hunter Plastics Limited
Nathan Way
London
SE28 0AE
Tel: 020 8855 9851

Marley Roofing Products

Mr. Mark Blewitt
c/o The National Federation of Roofing Contractors

Suppliers and Useful Addresses

United Kingdom

Axminster Power Tool Centre
Chard Street
Axminster
Devon EX13 5HU
Tel: 01297 33656
Power tools supplier

Black and Decker and Dewalt
210 Bath Road
Slough
Berkshire SL1 3YD
Tel: 01753 567055
Power tools supplier

Colour Centre
Offord Road
London N1
Tel: 020 7609 116
Paints and DIY equipment supplier

Foxell and James
Farringdon Road
London EC1M 3JB
Tel: 020 7405 0152
Wax, oil, varnish, and finishing products

Heward and Dean
Grove Park Road
London N15 4SP
Tel: 020 8800 3447
Tool supplier

HSS Power Tools
25 Willow Lane
Mitcham
Surrey CR4 4TS
Tel: 020 8260 3100

James Latham
Leeside Wharf
Mount Pleasant Hill
Clapton E5
Tel: 020 8806 3333
Timber suppliers

Plasplugs Ltd.
Wetmore Road
Burton-on-Trent
Staffordshire DE14 1SD
Tel: 01283 530303
www.plasplugs.com
Tiling tools, fixings and fasteners

Record Tools Ltd.
Parkway Works
Kettlebridge Road
Sheffield S9 3BL
Tel: 0114 244 9066
Hand tools supplier

Ronseal Limited
Thorncliffe Park
Chapeltown
Sheffield S35 2YP
Tel: 0114 246 7171
www.ronseal.co.uk
Ronseal, Colron, Thompson's products

Spear & Jackson
Neill Tools Ltd.
Atlas Way
Atlas North
Sheffield S4 7QQ
Tel: 0114 261 4242
Tools supplier

Stanley Tools UK Ltd.
Beighton Road East
Drakehouse
Sheffield S20 7JZ
Tel: 0114 276 8888
Tools supplier

Vitrex Ltd.
Everest Road
Lytham St. Annes
Lancashire
FY8 3AZ
Tel: 01253 789180
Tools and clothing

Woodfit Ltd.
Kem Mill
Whittle-le-Woods
Chorley
Lancashire PR6 7EA
Tel: 01257 266421
Furniture fittings supplier

United States

Compton Lumber & Hardware Inc.
P.O. Box 84972
Seattle, WA 98124-6272
Tel: (206) 623-5010
www.comptonlbr.com

Constantine's
2050 Eastchester Road
Bronx, New York NY 10461
Tel: (718) 792-1600
www.constantines.com

The Cutting Edge, Inc.
7123 Southwest Freeway
Houston, TX 77074
Tel: (981) 9228
www.cuttingedgetools.com

Northern Tool and Equipment
Corporate Headquarters
2800 Southcross Drive West
Burnsville, MN 55306
Tel: (800) 533-5545
www.northerntool.com

Australia
BBC Hardware Stores
Hardware House
For details of your nearest store
in either of the above two chains,
contact (02) 9876 0888

Mitre 10
For details of your nearest store
contact (03) 9703 4200

Bunnings Warehouse
For details of your nearest store
contact (03) 9607 0777

Thrifty-Link Hardware
See you local state directory for
your nearest store

Useful addresses
British Cement Association
Century House
Telford Avenue
Berkshire RG45 6YS
Tel: 01344 762676
www.bca.org.uk

**British Wood Preserving and
Damp-proofing Association**
1 Gleneagles House
Vernon Gate, South Street
Derby DE1 1UP
Tel: 01332 225100
www.bwpda.co.uk

**Conservatory Association/Glass
and Glazing Federation**
44–48 Borough High Street
London SE1 1XB
Tel: 01480 458278
www.ggf.org.uk

Energy Saving Trust
21 Dartmouth Street
London SW1H 9BT

Tel: 08457 277200
www.est.org.uk

Home Energy Efficiency Scheme
Eaga Partnership
2nd Floor, Eldon Court
Eldon Square
Newcastle-upon-Tyne NE1 7HA
Tel: 0800 316 6011

Kitchen Specialists Association
12 Top Barn Business Centre
Holt Heath
Worcester WR6 6NH
Tel: 01905 726066
www.ksa.co.uk

Laminated Glass Information Centre
299 Oxford Street
London W1R 1LA
020 7499 1720
www.martex.co.uk/prca/condor

**National Association of Loft
Insulation Contractors**
and
**National Cavity Insulation
Association**
PO Box 12
Hazlemere
Surrey GU27 3AH
Tel: 01428 654011
theceed@computer.com

National Fireplace Association
6th Floor
The McLaren Building
35 Dale End
Birmingham B4 7LN
Tel: 0121 200 1310

**RIBA (Royal Institute of
Chartered Architects)**
66 Portland Place
London W1B 1AD

Tel: 020 7580 5533
www.architecture.com

SALVO
(Directory of Salvage Yards)
PO Box 333
Cornhill on Tweed
Northumberland TD12 4YJ
Tel: 01890 820333
www.salvo.co.uk

**The Association of Noise
Consultants**
6 Trap Road
Guilden Morden
Hertfordshire SG8 0JE
Tel: 01763 852958
www.association-of-noise-
consultants.co.uk

**The Institute of Electrical
Engineers**
2 Savoy Place
London WC2R 0BL
Tel: 020 7240 1871
www.iee.org.uk

The Institute of Plumbing
64 Station Lane
Hornchurch
Essex RM12 6NB
Tel: 01708 472791
www.plumbers.org.uk

Index